All Scripture references taken from the KJV of the Holy Bible, unless otherwise indicated.

Bethesda: *Healing In God's Appointed Places*

by Dr. Marlene Miles

Freshwater Press 2025

freshwaterpress9@gmail.com

ISBN: 978-1-971933-11-5

Paperback Version

And there is water in heaven… rivers of Heaven,
flowing from the Throne of God.

Table of Contents

Bethesda

Healing In God's Appointed Places

By Dr. Marlene Miles

Freshwater Press, USA

Floating in the Dead Sea

I had a personal encounter with healing waters. I once floated in the Dead Sea. I was surrounded by those who traveled from around the world seeking relief, restoration, and hope. There, in the thick mineral waters that lift every weary body, I saw something profound: no one sinks. No matter the weight, no matter if it is seen or unseen, or if it is carried physically, emotionally, the water holds you up. It returns you to the surface again and again.

Standing among people who came for healing, I understood something deeper about the waters of Scripture: God's waters lift what life has pushed down. They restore what heaviness has tried to bury. That experience became a living metaphor—one that would later echo in the healing pools of the Bible. Those pools will be explored throughout this book.

Introduction

In the beginning, before any pool is named or described, there is water. Water in Scripture is never an accident. It is the symbol of the Spirit, the presence of God moving over chaos, the agent of cleansing, rebirth, healing, and transformation. Before there were cities, kingdoms, or temples, "the Spirit of God moved upon the face of the waters." This book begins there—at the place where God meets humanity in our deepest need.

The inspiration for this book was not merely an idea, but a calling. It was a spiritual whisper, a stirring, a divine invitation. I heard this word in my spirit, *Bethesda*. More than once and for more than one day or week, *Bethesda, Bethesda*. The theme of Bethesda and the pools of the Bible emerged like water rising from a hidden spring: quietly at first, then insistently, until it filled the landscape of my heart. Bethesda, the "House of Mercy," is more than a location in Jerusalem; it is a revelation of God's character. It is a doorway into understanding His desire to heal, restore, renew, save and keep His people alive and well.

Across the pages of Scripture, pools appear at moments where Heaven intersects with human suffering or human purpose. Sometimes these waters bring comfort. Sometimes they demand obedience. Sometimes they reveal truth. But always, they carry the redemptive heartbeat of God.

This book explores these waters: Bethesda, Siloam, Gibeon, Hezekiah's Pool, the desert pools, and baptismal waters and what they reveal about God's heart for healing. Each pool is a chapter in a larger story, a thread in a tapestry woven by the Holy Spirit. Together, they form a journey, a movement from brokenness toward restoration, from emptiness toward fullness, from waiting toward walking. At each pool there is a new revelation of God, who He is, how He works, and how He loves and proactively protects us, even from undeclared, unseen, and undercover things.

As you read, may you find your own story reflected in these waters. May these pages become a place of encounter. And may the God who still heals meet you where you are.

Reflection Questions

1. **What personal experiences have shaped your understanding of God's presence in your life?**

2. **Where do you feel God inviting you to begin a journey of healing and restoration?**

The Pools of the Bible

"Pools" in Scripture aren't random geographical features. These pools are tied to healing, cleansing, judgment, provision, and revelation. We know the Pool of Bethesda for the divine healing that happened there. The Pool of Siloam tells the story of sending and obedience, where a man's sight is restored. The Pool of Gibeon tells of conflict, confrontation, and human striving. The Pool of Hezekiah shows the foresight of God and how victory is assured when man prepares by God's instructions. It further speaks of preservation and wise stewardship. The Pool of Shur in the wilderness is about encounters during exile and wandering. This book connects these to reveal a *thread of spiritual symbolism.*

Bethesda is the anchor; it's the most well-known pool in the New Testament and we will spend most of our time there. It is there we recall the miraculous healing by Jesus, and embodies the heart of God's character: Mercy toward the broken. It sets the tone for a book about encountering God at the water's edge — whether for healing, clarity, repentance, or calling.

This book will move through Scripture, but also through the human heart, exploring each pool as a setting, a symbol, and a spiritual moment. We will see how others may have in their journey from need to healing and with clarity moved into obedience and then purpose, while offering a fresh lens for reading Scripture. We will focus on healing and restoration while we look at the Pool of Bethesda, especially.

Scripture mentions the following **pools**: Pools of Solomon, The Pool of Gibeon (2 Samuel 2:13). The Pool of Hebron (2 Samuel 4:12),. The upper pool at Jerusalem (2 Kings 18:17 20:20. We will mention briefly, the Pool of Samaria (1 Kings 22:38 KJV) .

The King's Pool (Nehemiah. 2:.14, 3:15, and Eccles. 2:6) we see that not every biblical pool was a place of healing. The Pool of Samaria (1 Kings 22:38) stands as a solemn reminder that water can also be a witness to judgment, fulfilling God's Word with unshakable certainty. While many pools in Scripture reveal God's Mercy and restoration, the Pool of Samaria (1 Kings 22:38) serves as a striking contrast. This one is not just about healing waters, but it testified to divine justice against an evil king. Yet we know that Ahab was one of the worst kings ever, and when the wicked cease to rule, the people rejoice. In that, we see a healing in the hearts and minds of a people because of that extreme evil ruler saw justice at God's hand.

The **Pool of Bethesda** is referred to in John's Gospel where Jesus healed a paralyzed man at a pool of water in Jerusalem. This pool is located at the Sheep Gate and is surrounded by five covered colonnades or porticos. It is also referred to as Bethzatha. It is now associated with the site of a pool in the current Muslim Quarter of the city, near the gate now called the Lions' Gate or St. Stephen's Gate and the Church of St. Anne, excavated in the late 19th century.

The name, *Bethesda* means either "House of Mercy" or "House of Grace." This meaning may have been thought appropriate, since the location was seen as a place of **disgrace** due to the presence of invalids. In those days the infirm, the invalids, lepers and the like were supposed to be outside the city, outside the gate and people did not even look at them. This is why an infirm person would cry out, "Look on Me, or look at me." It's why people asked the Lord to turn His countenance or face toward them.

By Grace, when she was exiled, Hagar realized that there is a God that will look on you – Jehovah Roi. There is a God who sits high and looks low at His Creation.

However, this place became a place, Bethesda of Grace due to the granting of healing.

Named the Sheep's Gate because it was alleged that this pool was a place where sheep were washed. However, popular stories say that the pool was not used to wash sheep because it was too deep.

We are His flock, the sheep of his pasture... so, it could stand to reason hat mankind should wash in the Pool of Bethesda; a pool of legendary healing.

The Power of Water

We all know the power of water or the power that water can wield when it is in force and has momentum. If we don't believe it, we will—in time. Water acts, it moves, it can destroy and without it there would be no life on this planet—at all. Water speaks; the Voice of the Lord is upon many waters. Water heals, it cleanses, it purifies and it marks transitions.

God uses water as a tool of Creation. The spirit moved over the face of the deep (the waters) (Genesis 1:2). Water was the canvas for creation.

God used water as a tool of Judgment & Renewal. The Flood (Genesis 6–8). We see how Pharaoh and his entire army were drowned in the Red Sea.

Water destroys *and* water renews.

He uses it as a tool of deliverance clearly seen in the Red Sea crossing where the Hebrews marched out of slavery. The Jordan River crossing was necessary because water had become the boundary between bondage and promise.

God used water as a tool of Healing. In the Old Testament, Naaman washed 7 times and was healed of leprosy. In the New Testament, by the Pool of Bethesda--, not in it, which we will go into in depth in this book. Jesus uses the Pool of Siloam where He miraculously healed a man who was born blind.

Water becomes a medium of recovery.

God used water as a tool of cleansing as indicated for the Levitical washings. He used it for ritual purification as well as for Priestly consecration.

Water separates the holy from the unclean.

God used water again as a tool of Covenant where John the Baptist baptized Jesus and where we are now baptized into Christ.

Water marks the new life.

God uses water as a tool of Judgment. God has complete control and command over the seas. Jesus has full authority to rebuke a storm. Jonah in his rebellion was swallowed in the depths.

Water is powerful *and it is obedient to God.*

It was used as a tool of Revelation when Jesus refers to "living water" when He is talking to the woman a the well. Then there is Ezekiel's river rising from the temple. Water symbolizes the Spirit's flow.

Water is an indicator of abundance: The River of God is full of water (Psalm 65:9).

In Scripture, water isn't just an element. It is a medium, a boundary, a separator, a signpost, a teacher, a servant of God's will, and often, a mirror of the soul.

But we don't worship it.

Water is also spiritually symbolic, representing the Holy Spirit, cleansing, life, power, transformation birthing, death and resurrection, refreshing, flow. It also represents God's presence and God's pleasure or displeasure with mankind. There is rain when He is pleased and drought when He is not. Drought is a curse.

Where water appears in the Bible, God is doing something powerful. Water has powers given by God: Power to cleanse--, not just physically, but ritually and symbolically. Power to carry Israel through the Red Sea, Noah in the ark. Power to separate dark from light, slavery from freedom, old season from new. Power to reveal who belongs to God (Jordan baptisms, ritual washings). Power to destroy floods, storms, chaotic waters. Power to heal Naaman, Bethesda, Siloam. Power to flow. Living water — the Holy Spirit. Power to respond to God. Waters part, stand still, rise, fall, obey. Power to birth. When a mother's water breaks it signals that it is time for birthing a new life.

Water has the power to symbolize everything from chaos to order, death to resurrection. Water is not just a background feature. It is an active participant in God's story.

Pools, waters, healing, restoration, movement, waiting, stepping in, obeying, encountering God at the water's edge are some of the ways God has instructed those or met those whom He has blessed. Often, people come to the water and look, when God is saying, "Get in." Most people want to feel close to healing, want to be near revival, want the atmosphere, sunbathe by the water, admire the water, *but never enter it.*

Bethesda's porches were full of people near the water. The Bible says there were a multitude of people there, but Jesus healed the one who engaged when He spoke. Moses had to stretch out his hand. Joshua had to step in. The priests had to touch the Jordan with their feet. Sometimes looking is not enough. Presence is not participation. Healing comes with obedience, with immersion, either in the water or in the Spirit, as the Lord directs.

Theological Clarification About Water & Healing

Water has been used across cultures and throughout history for cleansing, reflection, and renewal. In many places, water rituals—whether herbal baths, salt washes, or symbolic immersions—are practiced for spiritual, emotional, or energetic purposes. These traditions vary widely in meaning and intent.

This book, however, is concerned with biblical waters, waters appointed by God, visited by His presence, or used by His prophets, priests, apostles, and ultimately by Jesus Himself.

In Scripture, water is never the source of healing; **God is.** The Pool of Bethesda did not have the power, but God did, if God sent His angel to stir those waters, then it was God's power that healed. Not the water, not the angel. However, every angel is not from God, and the enemy of our souls also has "angels" that fell with him when he was cast out of Heaven. Not our focus in this book, but the devil has power and if he wants to use it for healing, be it real or fake, temporary of just assigned to another person and taken off the one who worships him, then that is how he will use it. If allowed, if the devil wants to use power to cause competition, disagreements, frustration, arguments --, any work of the flesh, then he will do it. What has this to do with a book about pools of the Bible? *Doesn't a predatory animal come to the water to seek prey?* Humans need water to live. Humans seek water for it's real, known, God-directed and legendary benefits. Water is made to serve man. So wouldn't the devil, a counterfeiter also find a counterfeit hidden way to use it for his own devices?

The Jordan River did not heal Naaman. It was Naaman's obedience to the Lord through the word of God given to the Prophet. The Pool of Siloam did not give sight; Jesus did. The Red Sea did not part itself—God moved and by His power the Sea parted so that the Hebrew slaves walked out of Egypt on dry land. Baptismal water in and of itself does not cleanse—Jesus cleanses.

Water is a symbol, a setting, a sign, a **place where God meets us**, but never a substitute for Him.

The purpose of this book is not to promote water rituals, techniques, or symbolic practices. It is to illuminate the ways God uses water in Scripture to reveal His Mercy, healing, renewal, restoration, transition, obedience, identity, and His presence among His people.

If you come from another background such as New Ageism, cultural ritual, ancestral tradition, or folk practices—you are welcome here. But understand that: **Healing in the Bible does not come from a method. It comes from a Person, and His name is Jesus.**

Spiritual Cleansing vs. Biblical Cleansing

Spiritual Cleansing (New Age, Metaphysical, Folk Belief)

Modern spirituality often speaks of *cleansing* in terms of energy removal, aura purification, vibration resetting, or releasing negative forces. This usually involves any combination of the following: salt baths, crystals, moon water, sage or incense, intention statements, visualization, symbolic washing, other herbs or minerals, breathing techniques, and or "releasing negative energy."

The idea behind these practices is that objects, elements, or ritual actions have inherent power to cleanse, protect, or shift the spiritual atmosphere around a person.

These practices focus on *self-generated purification*, using tools or steps to produce a desired spiritual state. This is not God and it is not God, but it can be so insidious that people don't think they are doing anything wrong--, even Christians are deceived by these things if they are not careful and discerning.

Biblical Cleansing

Biblical cleansing happens in the presence of God, not in the power of an object. In Scripture, God cleanses. Jesus sanctifies. The Holy Spirit renews. The Word washes. Repentance restores.

Water in Scripture symbolizes forgiveness, renewal, deliverance, healing, transition, and also obedience. But the power is never in the water itself. Biblical cleansing is not an atmosphere you create, but, instead, a work God performs. What Jesus did at the Pool of Bethesda was not about any of this.

Balneotherapy, Or Something More?

Hot springs, for example, have been used as **balneotherapy** to treat illness for centuries. Balneotherapy is a method of treating diseases by bathing, a traditional medicine technique usually practiced at spas. Since ancient times, humans have used hot springs, public baths and thermal medicine for therapeutic effects. While it is considered distinct from hydrotherapy, there are some overlaps in practice and in underlying principles.

So, the results also reflect that people with illnesses frequently go to hot springs to improve their symptoms. Most of those who come to divine pools, places of healing, and hot springs do so for the high mineral content in the waters. The mineral content is not the same everywhere, but it is basically the same daily in any given place, so there is no set time for a person seeking healing, recovery, or restoration to come to those springs or pools and be guaranteed relief or complete healing. There is no set time that an "angel" will come and make the water better, stronger, more potent or magical to enhance one's healing.

However, the Pool of Bethesda was alleged to be different. Legend had it that a healing angel would come and trouble or stir the water. Was that angel Raphael? The passage doesn't say, although he is the angel of healing. So it was said that the first one in the pool after the angel stirred it is the one that would be healed.

The name *Bethesda* appears in John 5:2–9, referring to the *Pool of Bethesda* in Jerusalem, known as a place of healing. The word itself is usually translated as "house of mercy" or "house of grace, " a name with ancient, sacred precedence, But was this special healing pool anything more than balneotherapy? Was it more than a mineral springs that would make the bather feel better because perhaps they were lacking magnesium, sulfur, or other essentials in their bodies, and those minerals were in the water in high concentrations?

The following is the Biblical account.

The Healing at Bethesda (John 5:1-)

After this there was a feast of the Jews; and Jesus went up to Jerusalem.

Now there is at Jerusalem by the sheep *market* a pool, which is called in the Hebrew tongue Bethesda, having five porches.

In these lay a great multitude of impotent folk, of
blind, halt, withered, waiting for the moving of the
water.

For an angel went down at a certain season into the
pool, and troubled the water: whosoever
then first after the troubling of the water stepped
in was made whole of whatsoever disease he had.

And a certain man was there, which had an
infirmity thirty and eight years.

When Jesus saw him lie, and knew that he had
been now a long time *in that case*, he saith unto
him, Wilt thou be made whole?

The impotent man answered him, Sir, I
have no man, when the water is
troubled, to put me into the pool: but while I am
coming, another steppeth down before me.

Jesus saith unto him, Rise, take
up thy bed, and walk.

And immediately the man was
made whole, and took
up his bed, and walked: and on the
same day was the sabbath.

The Jews therefore said unto him that was cured, It
is the sabbath day: it is not lawful for thee to
carry *thy* bed.

He answered them, He that made me whole, the
same said unto me, Take up thy bed, and walk.

Then asked they him, What man is that
which said unto thee, Take up thy bed, and walk?

And he that was healed wist not who it
was: for Jesus had conveyed himself away, a
multitude being in *that* place.

Afterward Jesus findeth him in the
temple, and said unto him, Behold, thou art
made whole: sin no more, lest a worse
thing come unto thee.

The man departed, and told the Jews that it
was Jesus, which had made him whole.

And therefore did the
Jews persecute Jesus, and sought to
slay him, because he had done these things on the
sabbath day.

At the Pool of Bethesda—near it, not in it,
Jesus came and spoke with the invalid man. First, He
spoke with the man, then He spoke to the man's spirit.
The man's spirit picked him up and he walked and then
also carried his bed. After 38 years, possible atrophy,
he walked and had strength also to carry his bed.

Jesus spoke to the man's spirit and that spirit
man had to obey Jesus. The spirit man obeys God; it's
Creator. All of Creation obeys the Word of God. All of
it, except those who willfully oppose Him. Willful
rebellion and disobedience will not go unnoticed,
unjudged, and unpunished, however.

The Porches

Historically, the Pool of Bethesda, near the Sheep Gate in Jerusalem was built as two adjacent pools with five covered colonnades, Four porches around the perimeter, One dividing porch between the two pools. There were five porches of Bethesda and they carry spiritual significance.

In John 5:2, the Pool of Bethesda is described as having five porches (porticos). These were shaded, columned walkways where the sick, blind, lame, and paralyzed gathered, hoping for healing.

Architecturally, the five porches existed because There were two adjacent pools separated by a central dividing porch, surrounded by four outer porches. But the deeper meaning isn't just architectural, it's prophetic, symbolic, and thematic.

Symbolic Meaning of the Number Five

In Scripture, the number 5 is consistently connected to Grace, Mercy, and God's compassionate provision. There are five books of the Torah (the foundation of God's covenant Grace). Five loaves fed the multitudes. There are the five-fold ministry gifts. There were 5 wounds of Christ. And we see offerings involving multiples of five. So, the "House of Mercy" (Bethesda) having five porches is no accident. It embodies God's invitation to Grace for the broken.

The Porches as Places of Waiting

Each porch sheltered people who were vulnerable, forgotten, hoping, waiting, desperate, stuck. The porches symbolize the spaces in our lives where we wait for God, even for years.

Each porch could represent a *different kind of human need*:

Porch 1 — The Waiting of the Hopeless - For people who have tried everything and have nothing left.

Porch 2 — The Waiting of the Overlooked - People who feel unseen or ignored (like the man who had "no one to help him").

Porch 3 — The Waiting of the Broken Body - Physical pain, chronic suffering, weakened flesh.

Porch 4 — The Waiting of the Broken Heart - Emotional wounds, abandonment, grief.

Porch 5 — The Waiting of the Broken Spirit - Loss of purpose, shattered identity, spiritual exhaustion.

The porches are gateways to restoration, Even though the porches were places of suffering, they were also the closest place to healing. Each porch represents part of the story of transformation: brokenness, proximity, encounter, command ("Rise, take up your bed, and walk"), Restoration. They are thresholds — places where the old life ends and the miracle begins.

The porches show that healing is not one-size-fits-all. Five porches could mean that society was getting sicker and sicker and they had to keep adding on for those who needed to come for healing or deliverance. Five porches = many people and many kinds of people. One Jesus = one source of healing. Each porch held a different mix of needs and stories, but Jesus healed the man personally, individually, directly — not through the pool. Jesus meets each person uniquely. Healing doesn't follow formulas. Grace is specific, not generic. Jesus knows exactly what you need and when you need it.

The porches prepare the way at Bethesda: healing in Mercy. Siloam: healing in obedience. Gibeon: healing in conflict. Hezekiah's Pool: healing through preparedness. Desert pools: healing in dryness. Baptismal waters: ultimate healing in Christ.

Bethesda introduces the *pattern* of waiting, brokenness, disappointment, divine encounter, and transformation. Later, we will see that the pools explore other dimensions of that same journey.

The Number of Grace (and why Bethesda had five porches) in Scripture, five is the number of Grace, favor, divine enablement, provision, and God's movement toward humanity. This makes the structure of Bethesda profoundly symbolic. The "House of Mercy" (Bethesda). Five Porches: the place where Grace meets human need. It means the architecture itself preached the message of the Messiah before Jesus ever walked into the scene.

In Bible times, the sick, the disabled, and lepers were often forced outside the community. In ancient Israel, there were strict purity laws (Leviticus 13–15) that required lepers to live outside the camp or outside city walls. Anyone considered "unclean" had to stay away from public worship. People with certain illnesses or disabilities could not enter in and they had to avoid physical contact with others. The infirm sat at gates, markets, roadsides, or along temple steps. This wasn't because they were "hated," but because ritual purity was required for temple worship, and disease was poorly understood. But the effect was the same; they were isolated, avoided, overlooked, and marginalized.

Passersby often avoided eye contact, especially with, lepers, beggars, the disabled, anyone "unclean," and those obviously afflicted.

Why?

Because people believed that touching them would make *you* ritually unclean. And they believed that God was judging them. To them, illness = sin—either that person's or a parent or ancestor. (Who sinned, this man or his parents?) They believed that a disability was the result of a curse and suffering was because of God's displeasure. Remember this was during the time of polytheism and those who served "other" *gods* were always treading carefully as not to anger or fail to worship that idol *god*, because if they didn't worship their idols, there would be punishments.

Beggars were socially shameful, so the culture around them was to avert your eyes, keep your distance, don't engage. The goal was to maintain ritual purity.

The one exception was when people tossed coins at them. This was not kindness, but obligation, so they could say they were faithful in almsgiving, or they gave to the poor.

Invalids were invisible to society, But not to Jesus. The very people society avoided, Jesus moved toward them. Jesus did the opposite of His culture because the culture was wrong. Jesus *saw* the invisible, looked for the lost and forgotten, dined with tax collectors and prostitutes, and sought the disabled.

The gate was a place of both exclusion and divine appointments. Those sitting outside the gate often had to beg for survival because they couldn't work. They were ignored or avoided. They had to rely on the mercy of others, even strangers. They had no community involvement and lived with shame and stigma.

The gate was also significant spiritually. It was the meeting place where Jesus found the ones everyone else walked past.

Bethesda was one such place — like an open-air hospital where people lay powerless. There, others stepped over them. Even when the water was stirred, the strong got ahead of the weak

So, that is precisely where Jesus walked.

Jesus, being filled with the Holy Spirit, certainly had divine appointments. He surely went where He was supposed to go. He went to God's appointed places. God's appointed waters. Places of God's appointed Love and Mercy. In His ministry, Jesus went to places and people appointed for healing.

It's as though these invalids were placed "outside the gate"—outside of the eye gates of people who walked past and never looked at them, —but *God Himself* came to meet them there.

In Bible times, the broken and infirm were pushed to the margins — outside the gate, outside the city, outside the flow of community life. But those very places became the stages where Jesus, keeping divine appointments and moving in divine power, revealed His compassion most clearly.

Bethesda — The House of Mercy

Bethesda is introduced in the Gospel of John with a single, powerful line: *"Now there is in Jerusalem near the Sheep Gate a pool, which in Aramaic is called Bethesda and which is surrounded by five covered colonnades."* (John 5:2). With this simple description, Scripture opens a doorway into one of the most symbolic and spiritually charged locations in the New Testament.

The name Bethesda means "House of Mercy" or "House of Grace." It is mercy not as an abstract idea, but as a place—tangible, visible, and accessible to the broken. For centuries, people gathered under its five porches, seeking relief from sickness, paralysis, blindness, and pain. These porches became sanctuaries for those whom society had cast aside. Here, the forgotten waited. The overlooked waited. The desperate waited.

Yet the story of Bethesda is not primarily about the water. It is about the One who walked into that space— a place filled with human suffering—and transformed it by His presence.

A Place of Waiting

The man Jesus encountered had been sick for thirty-eight years. His story represents every long-term struggle, every unanswered prayer, every season when healing feels impossibly out of reach. Bethesda reveals the emotional weight of waiting: the frustration, the longing, the disappointment of watching others step ahead while you remain stuck.

At Bethesda, Jesus does not ask the man about his past. He does not condemn him for his weakness. Instead, He asks a deeply personal question: *"Do you want to be made well?"* This question cuts through layers of despair and invites the man—and every reader—into a moment of honest desire and renewed hope.

The Significance of 38 Years

The detail that the man waited thirty-eight years is not accidental. In Scripture, the number 38 echoes Israel's long season of wandering (Deuteronomy 2:14). It symbolizes prolonged delay, cycles that refused to break, dreams deferred, seasons of almost there, and human effort exhausted. (Much more on this later.)

The man at Bethesda was not simply sick—he was stuck. Thirty-eight years marks the end of human ability and the moment when only divine mercy can break the cycle. Jesus meets him *precisely* at the point where self-effort dies and Grace begins.

Looking at the Water vs. Stepping Into It

Many came to Bethesda to be near the water, but few entered at the moment of stirring. This reveals a spiritual truth: people are often content to stand near hope without engaging it. Today we see the same pattern. Crowds flock to beaches simply to *be* near the water, to watch it, feel its presence, or admire its beauty. But fewer actually enter the water.

In Scripture, God often requires movement. Moses had to stretch out his hand over the sea. Joshua had to step into the Jordan before it parted. The priests carrying the ark had to place their feet in the water first. The principle is clear: breakthrough requires participation. It is not enough to look at the water— God calls us to step in. Healing begins where obedience meets immersion.

Grace That Comes to Us

Bethesda's five porches are not simply architectural details—they symbolize the fullness of God's grace. Long before Jesus arrived, the very structure of the place preached a message: *Grace surrounds the broken.* The porches sheltered those who could not help themselves, pointing to a deeper truth: in Christ, healing is not earned; it is received.

The man at Bethesda could not reach the water. He had no one to help him. His miracle came not because he made it to the pool, but because Jesus came to him. At Bethesda, Grace is not something you strive toward. It is Someone who steps toward you. If Grace were the theme of the day the many people on five porches would not still be waiting day after day; they would already be healed.

Rise, Take Up Your Bed, and Walk

With a single command, Jesus redefines what is possible: *"Rise, take up your bed, and walk."* Healing is not only a moment of restoration; it is a call into a new way of living. The bed that once held the man becomes the testimony he carries. What once symbolized limitation now becomes a symbol of transformation. This is a reversal of authority, where the bed had authority over the man, now the man has authority over the bed. Where the bed said you can go here, but not there--, Bethesda Man now says where the bed can go or not go. For all we knew he took it to the dumpster or burned it in a landfill.

In this first pool, Bethesda, we see the pattern that will guide the rest of the book. We see human need. We see a divine encounter. We hear a word spoken by God, and we see a response of faith. Finally, there is full deliverance, restoration and transformation. In those words that Jesus spoke can you see how words fitly spoken, even simple words of encouragement can lift a person so much, versus no words, or words of discouragement. Exhort your fellow man and tell him that he can do it, he can rise, and he can be successful in life. In so doing, you also hear those words and faith comes by hearing. Amen.

Bethesda is the gateway. It is where mercy meets us in our deepest need, where grace reaches the unreachable, and where healing begins.

Reflection Questions

1. **In what areas of your life have you felt "stuck" or overlooked?**

_____

_____

_____

_____

_____

_____

2. **What does the question "Do you want to be made well?" mean to you personally?**

_____

_____

_____

3. How might God be inviting you to step into healing rather than simply wait near it?

Siloam — The Pool of *Sending*

If Bethesda reveals the Mercy of Jesus toward the broken, Siloam reveals His purpose for the healed. The Pool of Siloam appears in John 9 during one of the most profound miracles in the New Testament: the healing of the man who had been blind from birth.

Where Bethesda highlights Grace coming *to* us, Siloam highlights Grace working *through* us. At Bethesda, Jesus asks, "Do you want to be made well?" At Siloam, Jesus gives a command that tests the heart: *"Go, wash in the Pool of Siloam."* (Which John interprets for us: "Siloam means '*sent.*'")

Healing Through Obedience

The miracle at Siloam unfolds not in the moment Jesus speaks, but in the man's response. With mud still covering his eyes, the blind man must navigate his way through the streets of Jerusalem. He cannot yet see the road. He cannot see the destination.

But he obeys.

Healing at Siloam is tied to obedience in motion. It is the kind of obedience that walks even when the path is unclear and moves before the miracle manifests. This faith-filled obedience trusts the voice of Jesus more than the evidence of the moment.

This pool teaches us that restoration is sometimes a journey. God often heals us as we go. In many cases, the breakthrough comes *in the walking,* not the waiting.

A Pool With a Mission

Siloam was part of Jerusalem's ancient water system, designed to channel water from the Gihon Spring into the city. It sustained life, refreshed pilgrims, and supported temple worship. Its name— *Sent*—reflects both its purpose and its spiritual message.

Just as water was sent into the city, Jesus sends His disciples into the world. Siloam becomes a living metaphor of purpose, commissioning, active faith and obedience with movement.

Bethesda gathers the broken. Siloam releases the *healed.* This is the rhythm of discipleship: we receive so we can be *sent.*

Seeing for the First Time

When the man washes in Siloam, his sight is restored. But the miracle is deeper than physical vision. Siloam represents the moment when God opens our eyes to identity, purpose, calling, and Truth. After healing comes clarity. After Mercy comes mission. After restoration comes revelation.

The journey from Bethesda to Siloam reflects the journey of every believer. We move from being healed by Christ to becoming vessels for Christ.

A New Way Forward

Siloam teaches us that healing is not the end—it's the beginning. When God restores us, He sends us. When He opens our eyes, He gives us a path to walk. The restored are not meant to remain in the shadow of the porches; they are meant to carry their testimony into the world.

Siloam is the water of purpose. It reminds us that every healing carries a calling.

Reflection Questions

1. **What act of obedience is God asking you to take, even before you see the result?**

2. **How does "walking it out" strengthen your faith?**

Where Conflict Reveals the Heart

If Bethesda is the place of Mercy and Siloam the place of sending, Gibeon is the place of conflict. It is a pool embedded in the story of Israel's struggle, a place where tension, confrontation, and the painful realities of human nature are brought into the light.

The Pool of Gibeon appears in 2 Samuel 2, during the turbulent transition between the reign of Saul and the rise of David. Israel was fractured. Loyalties were divided. The nation was standing at a crossroads. And at the edge of a quiet pool, the true condition of the human heart was revealed.

A Meeting at the Water's Edge

The scene opens with Joab and the servants of David arriving at Gibeon, while Abner and the servants of Saul's son, Ish-bosheth, arrive from the opposite side. Both groups meet at the pool—not by coincidence, but by divine orchestration. Gibeon becomes a stage where unresolved tension surfaces.

The pool, usually a place of refreshment and reflection, becomes the backdrop for confrontation. Water often represents peace, but here, it reveals the unrest within the hearts of men. Conflict does not arise from the water; it rises from within them.

The Sword Drawn

The tragic contest that follows—twelve men against twelve—reflects the futility of human pride. The Pool of Gibeon becomes a symbol of how quickly the human heart can turn toward violence, and how conflict among God's people wounds everyone.

This pool teaches us an important truth: conflict exposes what peace conceals.

At Gibeon, the hidden rivalries and unresolved hurt between the houses of Saul and David erupt into violence, revealing the deeper spiritual reality that Israel was a divided nation long before any sword was drawn.

God's Presence in the Midst of Struggle

Though Gibeon is a place of conflict, it is not a place abandoned by God. In fact, God often leads us to places like Gibeon to do heart work that cannot be done in places like Bethesda or Siloam.

At Gibeon, we learn that God meets us even in our conflict. And that healing sometimes requires confrontation. Restoration often demands that truth be faced.

Gibeon confronts us with the uncomfortable reality that broken relationships, unresolved issues, and internal battles must be addressed if we are to move forward in wholeness.

The Journey Through Conflict

The Pool of Gibeon is an invitation to reflect on our own struggles. We should evaluate those moments when the water is still but our hearts are turbulent. Conflict is not the end of the story; it is often the beginning of transformation.

God allows us to stand at our own Gibeons so He can expose what needs healing, reveal areas of pride or fear, bring us into deeper unity and maturity, and then lead us to forgiveness and reconciliation

Peace After the Storm

Although Gibeon is marked by violence, it ultimately points toward peace. The struggle between the Houses of Saul and David does not last forever. God brings resolution, unity, and a new season for Israel. Gibeon teaches us that conflict is not meant to destroy us but to purify us.

In the journey of healing, conflict is sometimes the necessary doorway to deeper peace.

Reflection Questions:

1. What conflicts—internal or external—are revealing deeper truths in your heart?

_____

_____

_____

_____

_____

2. How have past struggles shaped your current spiritual journey?

_____

_____

_____

_____

_____

The King's Pool — Seeing Brokenness Honestly

The King's Pool is mentioned in the Book of Nehemiah as part of his nighttime inspection of Jerusalem's broken walls. Unlike Bethesda or Siloam, there is no miracle recorded here. There is no dramatic healing, no sudden breakthrough, no divine intervention in that moment. Instead, the King's Pool becomes the backdrop for something just as crucial: honest assessment.

Healing cannot begin until brokenness is acknowledged. Restoration cannot occur until ruin is seen clearly. The King's Pool is where God invites us to look at what has been damaged in our lives—not to shame us, but to prepare us for renewal.

A Night Journey Through Ruins

Nehemiah arrives in Jerusalem with a God-given mission, but before he gathers workers or announces a plan, he walks alone at night. He visits the King's Pool and examines the ruined walls by the dim light of the moon. Some areas are so broken that his horse cannot pass through.

This scene is deeply symbolic. Darkness forces Nehemiah to rely on more than sight; he must move carefully, thoughtfully, prayerfully. In the same way, God often leads us into quiet, reflective seasons where He shows us the truth about our condition. This is not to overwhelm us, but to prepare us.

The King's Pool teaches us that awareness precedes restoration.

Seeing What Others Ignore

For years, the people of Jerusalem had lived among the ruins. Broken walls had become normal. The destruction around them no longer stirred urgency. But when Nehemiah saw the damage, he responded with righteous determination.

There are places in our hearts and lives where brokenness has become familiar. We learn to step over rubble. We adjust to the gaps. We make peace with what is unfinished or damaged. The King's Pool invites us to take a deeper look and see what God wants to rebuild.

A Pool of Vision

Though nothing miraculous happens at the King's Pool, everything that happens afterward is made possible because of this moment. Vision is birthed here. Calling becomes clear here. The plan for restoration begins here.

This pool represents discernment, truth-telling, honest evaluation, and the courage to face reality.

Before God rebuilds, He reveals. Before He restores, He shines a light on the broken places.

The God Who Rebuilds

Nehemiah does not despair when he sees the ruin. Instead, he is stirred to action. The King's Pool teaches us that seeing brokenness is never meant to leave us hopeless; it is meant to give us clarity of purpose. It is a holy moment when God aligns our hearts with His desire to restore.

This chapter reminds us that, with God, what is broken is not beyond repair. What is ruined is not beyond redemption. What has crumbled can be rebuilt by God's hand or by our own hand with God's help.

The King's Pool prepares us for the miraculous, for the rebuilding, and for the renewal that only God can accomplish.

Reflection Questions:

1. **What broken areas in your life are you being called to examine with honesty?**

_____

_____

_____

_____

_____

_____

_____

2. How can facing the truth be the first step toward rebuilding?

_____

_____

_____

_____

_____

_____

_____

Hezekiah's Pool — Prepared for the Unexpected

Hezekiah's Pool represents wisdom, foresight, and spiritual preparedness. While other pools in Scripture highlight healing, confrontation, or commissioning, this pool speaks of God's protection through strategic obedience. It reminds us that healing is not only about what God does in a moment, but what He empowers us to prepare for in seasons.

A Pool Built for Preservation

King Hezekiah faced an impending threat: the Assyrian empire—a force known for its cruelty and overwhelming military strength. Jerusalem was vulnerable. Its water sources lay outside the city walls, exposed to enemy control.

Rather than ignore the danger or panic in fear, Hezekiah acted with Wisdom and submission to God's guidance. He redirected the Gihon Spring through an underground tunnel. This is one of the greatest engineering feats of the ancient world, bringing water safely inside the city to what became known as Hezekiah's Pool. This was not a moment of crisis reaction; it was preparation for God's deliverance.

Faith That Plans Ahead

Hezekiah's Pool teaches us that faith is not passive. Faith listens. Faith discerns. Faith prepares. There are moments when God calls us to take steps that make little sense to others but are vital to our future. Didn't He do that with Noah? Didn't the people laugh and mock?

Preparation is not fear; it is stewardship.

God often alerts us to coming challenges. He gives us strategies to protect what He is building in us. He leads us to strengthen weak areas before pressure arrives. He guides us to create reservoirs of spiritual, emotional, or practical strength. Didn't He do that with Joseph, during the seven years of plenty, preparing the entire area for the seven years of famine?

Strength Beneath the Surface

What makes Hezekiah's Pool so compelling is that much of the work was hidden underground. The tunnel was carved through bedrock, unseen but essential.

God often does His most important preparatory work beneath the surface: Deepening our character. Strengthening our faith. Expanding our resilience. Rooting our identity in Him.

By the time the Assyrian army arrived, the city had a secure water supply. The pool stood as visible proof of invisible obedience.

A sidebar here, if God does that, and the enemy of our souls copies God, then wouldn't a lot of what the devil does be underground. This is why we need a strong walk with the Lord, a real prayer life, a fortified connection with the Holy Spirit and keen discernment.

When Preparation Meets Miracle

In the end, it was God, not Hezekiah, who defeated the Assyrians. One angel brought deliverance that no amount of human planning could have accomplished. Yet Hezekiah's preparation played a crucial role in sustaining the city through the siege.

God uses both our obedience and His intervention to bring victory.

Hezekiah's Pool shows us that healing often involves preparation, setting things in order, strengthening what remains, and cooperating with God to fortify our lives for challenges we cannot yet see.

A Reservoir of Grace

For the believer, Hezekiah's Pool symbolizes readiness, resilience, God-led strategy, protection, and partnership between divine power and human obedience. This pool invites us to ask: *What is God calling me to prepare today that will sustain me tomorrow?* It reminds us that restoration is not only something God does for us, it is something He builds within us.

Reflection Questions:

1. **What is God asking you to prepare for in this season?**

_____

_____

_____

_____

_____

_____

_____

_____

_____

2. **Can you name something that the Lord had you to do to prepare for something in your life, but others thought you were**

**weird or off your rocker? What did you
learn or how did you grow from that?**

_____

_____

_____

_____

_____

_____

3. **What "beneath the surface" work is He
doing in you right now?**

_____

_____

_____

_____

_____

_____

_____

Desert Pools — Water in Wilderness Places

The desert is one of Scripture's most consistent metaphors for seasons of testing, dryness, and disorientation. Yet it is in the wilderness that some of the most profound revelations of God occur. The desert strips away distractions, familiar comforts, and false securities, leaving us face-to-face with our need for God.

It is in the wilderness that God provides unexpected pools, moments of divine provision, encounters of refreshing Grace, and waters that appear where none should exist. These pools teach us that God is not absent in barren places; He is intimately present, leading us step by step.

A God Who Sees in the Desert

One of the earliest desert pools in Scripture is the encounter between Hagar and God in Genesis 16 and again in Genesis 21. Cast out, exhausted, and alone, Hagar collapses under the weight of despair. In the heat of the wilderness, she believes death is inevitable for her and her son.

But God hears the cry of the boy. The Angel of the Lord calls to Hagar and opens her eyes to a well of water she had not seen before. The desert did not change—but Hagar's vision did.

Desert pools are often wells of provision we never noticed until God opened our eyes.

These waters teach us that God hears us when we feel unseen. God provides even when we feel forgotten. God reveals hidden resources at just the right time. Hagar names God *El Roi*—"The God who sees me." The desert becomes a place of revelation.

Sweet Waters After Bitter Seasons

Israel's journey through the wilderness highlights another desert pool: the waters of Marah and Elim (Exodus 15). After crossing the Red Sea, the people travel three days without water, only to find bitter, undrinkable water at Marah. Their hope turns to frustration.

But God transforms the bitter into the sweet. He leads them from Marah to Elim, where twelve springs and seventy palm trees provide abundant rest.

These desert waters show us that bitter seasons are not permanent and God can transform what disappoints us into something lovely. We can see that His provision is often just beyond the trial, and rest awaits those who continue the journey.

The wilderness is not the end, it is the passageway. Don't despise the journey you're on; despise the journey you missed.

Streams in the Wasteland

Through Isaiah, God gives a promise that echoes through every wilderness season: *"I will make a way in the wilderness and rivers in the desert."* (Isaiah 43:19). This is more than poetry—it is a declaration of God's nature.

Desert pools represent hope in hopeless places. It illuminates His provision without explanation. These pools reveal Jehovah Jireh. It shows the miraculous in the mundane, and most of all, God's strength in human weakness. When everything around us looks barren, God creates paths and pours out water.

The Formation of Faith

The desert is not a punishment; it is a classroom. Many of God's greatest leaders such as Moses, David, Elijah, John the Baptist, even Jesus, were shaped in wilderness places. These seasons cultivate dependence on God, spiritual resilience, clarity of calling, and purity of heart. The desert reveals who we are and who God is.

When the Wilderness Becomes a Well

Desert pools teach us that God is faithful in every season. They remind us that even in the driest moments, He is present, leading us toward renewal, refreshment, and deeper intimacy with Him.

In the wilderness, God does not abandon us; instead, He sustains us. He supplies us with hidden wells, unexpected pools, and living water that restores the soul.

Reflection Questions:

1. **Where do you feel spiritually dry or in need of refreshment?**

2. **What unexpected provisions has God already provided in your wilderness seasons?**

Baptismal Waters — Rebirth and Renewal

Among all the waters of Scripture, none carries the weight of transformation quite like the waters of baptism. While Bethesda reveals Mercy, Siloam reveals obedience, Gibeon reveals conflict, the King's Pool reveals honest assessment, Hezekiah's Pool reveals preparation, desert waters reveal God's provision. Baptismal waters reveal new creation. While not a pool, *per se*, a mother's *water* announces new life.

Baptism is not merely symbolic; it is spiritual, covenantal, and deeply rooted in God's redemptive story. It is the moment when the old passes away, the new emerges, and a believer publicly identifies with the death, burial, and resurrection of Jesus Christ.

The Waters of New Beginning

Throughout Scripture, water marks the beginning of something new. It was present in Creation: The Spirit hovers over the waters. With Noah and the Ark, the Earth is purified through the flood. Moses: Israel passes through the Red Sea into their new identity. They were no longer slaves to Egypt but were now Israelites. Joshua: Israel crosses the Jordan into promise, into the Promised Land.

Baptism continues this pattern of new beginnings. It signifies that what once was has died, and what now is has been born by the Spirit.

Buried and Raised with Christ

Paul describes baptism as a participation in the death and resurrection of Jesus (Romans 6:3–4). The believer goes down into the water, identifying with the death of the old self, and rises to walk in newness of life. This is more than ritual. It is a declaration of faith, a renunciation of the old life, and a public testimony of inward Grace. It is a spiritual watershed moment

Through baptism, we proclaim that we are no longer defined by sin, shame, or the past. We are defined by Christ.

The Jordan River: A River of Destiny

Baptism is intimately connected to the Jordan River—the place where Jesus Himself was baptized by John. When Jesus entered the Jordan, He sanctified the waters for all who would follow. The heavens opened, the Spirit descended, and the Father spoke: *"This is My beloved Son."*

This moment reveals profound truths:

- Baptism is an affirmation of identity
- It is an anointing for purpose
- It is a moment of divine affirmation

Just as Jesus arose from the Jordan empowered by the Spirit, believers emerge from baptism marked for mission.

A Sign of Belonging

Baptism brings believers into a community of faith. It is both personal and communal—an individual act within the larger Body of Christ. It marks the transition from seeker to disciple, from wandering to belonging, from old identity to new covenant family.

Living the Baptized Life

The waters of baptism call us not only to a moment of transformation but to a lifestyle of renewal. It is the daily practice of dying to self, rising in Grace, walking in the Spirit, and embracing the call of God. Baptismal waters remind us that healing is not just about being restored; it is about becoming new.

The Culmination of All Waters

In many ways, this pool ties together all the others. At Bethesda we see Divine Mercy. At Siloam we truly understand the importance of obedience. At Gibeon there is refinement. At the King's Pool, there is awareness. We are reminded of the necessity for preparation by Hezekiah's Pool. The desert pools bring provision.

All these lead us to the ultimate water— rebirth. Baptism invites us to step fully into the life God has prepared, washed by His Mercy, empowered by His Spirit, and renewed in His image.

Reflection Questions:

1. **What old identity is God inviting you to release?**

2. **What new identity is He calling you to step into?**

How Did Bethesda Man Get to the Pool?

If the man by the Pool at Bethesda who I am now calling Bethesda Man couldn't get into the water, how did he get to the pool? The following are possibilities.

Bethesda Man was *carried there daily* by others — but they didn't stay to help him actually get into the water. This is the most historically likely scenario. In Jerusalem, the disabled were often carried by family, dropped off near gates, left near temple courts, placed in public areas, and or positioned where charity was expected.

People carried him to Bethesda…but no one stayed long enough to help him in when the water stirred. This explains his painful statement, "I have no man to put me into the pool." (John 5:7). Bethesda Man had *helpers* in the general sense, but not advocates.

He had people willing to drop him off, but not committed to stay with him. If they had work to do or somewhere to be, how could they sit by this pool all day, day after day, not knowing when or if the angel would trouble the water—that day? That week? That month? Or ever? Maybe those who helped him there or dropped him off didn't believe in this angel moving the water thing. Maybe they thought it was stupid, like a lottery and only one person could win their healing, when or *if* this invisible angel came. *Maybe?*

Perhaps they had sat with him previously and began to think this was a waste of time. This man's life was marked by abandonment, not total isolation.

Maybe Bethesda Man could walk *a little* or crawl, but not fast enough to reach the water before the winner – whoever that winner would be – that year, or that time. The Bible says season, so it may have only been once per year or four times in a year, or by some other definition of season.

"*Impotent*" is from the Greek: *asthenéō*. This does not always mean totally paralyzed--, it could mean simply weak or feeble. It could mean without strength, or differently abled, chronically disabled. If he could only crawl or drag himself, shuffle slowly, or maybe walk with a limp or with extreme difficulty he wouldn't win the prize of being healed in this *season*.

Seems he could arrive at the pool because he had *some* mobility, but when the rush--, when the competitive moment came, everyone else outpaced him, for 38 years. So, his disability didn't keep him away from Bethesda—it kept him from receiving breakthrough within the system, that was Bethesda at that time.

Perhaps he lived *very* close to the pool. Some people lived near the temple areas or public water sources because there, charity was available. Perhaps food handouts happened there. It was probably busy there; people came and went, but his people didn't stay with him. They may have dropped him off, and *went.*

He may have lived in a beggar's shelter or structure nearby, only needing minimal mobility to get to the pool when they thought the angel would come and stir the water – because how did they know when this stirring would happen? So, those who were most desperate probably came every day and wasted many days, weeks, months, and in the cases of Bethesda Man—many years waiting for his miracle. But getting into the water at the right moment? That required strength, speed, help, and all the things he lacked.

This reveals a story not about a physically stuck man, but as much about a man stuck in a system that had failed him—for 38 years.

He was almost there. He could get *near* mercy, but could not *reach* it. He could get *to* the edge, but not *into* the breakthrough. He lived close to hope, but that hope was dashed when someone else got into the pool before him. For 38 years, he watched others get healed, but not himself. He got to the place of healing, but he couldn't access it.

Once there, the man could have been afraid. The system whereby he could be healed was dangerous, treacherous and it was flesh-works producing. If Bethesda Man fell into the water and he wasn't first, or if he has mistakenly thought the angel had stirred the water, but the angel hadn't and there were no supernatural properties in that water, he might drown—depending on his ability to swim or tread water.

The pool was deep. ancient *mikveh*-style pools and public reservoirs were not shallow; they could be 10–15 feet deep in places. As we all know, even now, stone steps are slippery when wet. There were no railings, no lifeguards. Maybe the predominance of people there were disabled and couldn't help themselves, so how could they help another? There was probably no one to rescue someone who fell wrong. For a disabled man, getting into the water *incorrectly* could result in slipping, sinking, drowning. He could even risk being trampled by others rushing in.

In Scripture, his disability involves severe motor weakness. Even if he crawled or shuffled, once he lost his footing in water if he couldn't swim, stand, push himself up, tread water, or move quickly, he could lose his very life. The same water that healed the first person could kill the rest. So, for 38 years, it may not have been his hesitation that kept him from being healed; it may not have been laziness; it could have been survival instinct.

And there is fear of another kind: Fear of *false hope*. After 38 years, hope becomes dangerous.

Being disappointed repeatedly wears down the soul. At some point, "trying again" feels like a threat, not an opportunity. So yes, he feared falling, failing, flailing. He could have feared trying and losing again, the humiliation, the shame and despair. Sometimes deep fear makes us afraid to hope again. Hope deferred makes the heart sick.

But Jesus. Jesus removes BOTH the danger AND the despair for or from Bethesda Man. He doesn't say, "Let Me help you into the water." He says, **"Rise." "Take up your bed." "Walk."** Jesus bypasses all fear, competition, danger, and the need of a helper. Jesus removes every risk. Jesus removes the old system, entirely. He heals without asking the man to risk his life. This is a picture of Mercy and Grace.

It could be that Bethesda Man wasn't only afraid of being last; he was afraid of drowning. The place that promised healing also threatened harm. Jesus did not call him into danger—He called him into life. At that time, the Pool of Bethesda was used to offer a miracle to one and fear to all the rest. Jesus removed both the fear and the favoritism.

This gets deeper, *if* someone had stayed to help him get into the pool, but he didn't get healed, Bethesda Man could pull that helper down into the water as well, and they'd both could be drowned. The pool was deep enough that two weak or off-balance people could drown together. If his friend, relative, or helper lost their footing, slipped, was pulled down or was weighed down by the man's body, or got caught in the rush they BOTH could drown or be killed by trampling, by those that could run.

If you were a disabled comrade, helping him meant risking your own chance at healing.

So, the system at the Pool of Bethesda created self-preservation, competition, hesitation and maybe other flesh works such as covetousness, envy, jealousy, guile, malice, and even fights. One may say to another, "I'm sorry, but I can't help you — I might miss my own healing." In this environment, compassion becomes costly because ultimately, there was only enough for one. Does this sound like the kind of environment that God would create? Of course not.

Jesus, on the other hand healed every single person who asked for healing in the Gospels. Everyone. Jesus said that He desires that not one should be lost. This system at Bethesda needed to be upgraded.

God is not the author of confusion

This explains why Jesus stands out so radically. Jesus breaks the entire culture of scarcity. We serve a God of more than enough, El Shaddai.

As a kid hearing this story in Sunday School we always thought something was wrong with this man who was there for 38 years, like he was lazy or something. Perhaps he was not. Perhaps it was the system that was wrong, ineffective and did not bring honor to God, and promoted disunity and possibly resentment and bitterness in those who were there and in need. Jesus came and died for every man and God offers salvation to everyone and redemption from the Curse of the Law and that redemption includes healing. This means healing for all, every person, not just one.

Could it be that the power that stirred the water was only strong enough to heal one? If so, we should question that power. Our God is the greatest power; in Him is no weakness.

Bethesda Man had answered Jesus saying what he needed. The invalid man said, "I have no man." He wasn't just saying, "I have no friends." He was saying, "No one is willing to risk themselves for me."

He was near the pool, and the healing was in the 'pool – hit or miss – and we know Our Father is not hit or miss, but even in that system there was a gap, a chasm that the man in his own acts and humanity couldn't cross to the place of healing. He needed a man to be his Helper. He needed something more than what he was to get to where he wanted and needed to be.

Helping him meant possibly dying with him. If he panicked in the water… If he grabbed the helper…If he flailed or became erratic… If he lost stability… They'd BOTH go under. He needed a man, a friend that would be willing to risk everything for the sake of his friend, Bethesda Man.

This is why people brought him and laid him near the water, gave charity, wished him well, but they did not stay. If that man came there every day and did not work, if people sat with him, they also would not work. The Bible says that he who doesn't work should not eat. So, not staying was not cruelty, it was pragmatism. It could have been fear of losing productivity, time, money, livelihood, and life itself.

Not only that, due to Jewish customs and laws, how could a healthy person sit with infirm, disabled, sick, or diseased people by the gate, or in any place in public? That just wasn't done.

Ultimately, Bethesda Man had to realize that any *helpers* were only human.

What Jesus did is even MORE miraculous in light of this. Jesus didn't push him or take him to the water. Jesus didn't wait for an angel. Jesus didn't send thoughts and prayers and platitudes. Jesus didn't even require anything of this man – no performance.

Instead, Jesus eliminated the need for the water entirely. He bypassed the fear, the danger, the competition, every risk, the risk of drowning and even the wait. Jesus bypassed—no He surpassed the system that was in place and healed Bethesda Man. He said, **"Rise." "Take up your bed." "Walk."**

What Was This Pool?

Jesus healed everyone who asked. Where in the Bible is there another example of several people having a need, but only **one** received? Did Jesus not feed the multitude and not just one. Even when the little boy with the fishes in the loaves was just one, Jesus multiplied the food to feed all. This is God's way.

The Pool of Bethesda is the most direct example where there are many sick people who are disabled, lying around the same place while only one received healing at a time. This was religion in the sense that it was a system, and people did the same thing day after day with no real results. And, it is religion in the sense that those in charge, Pharisees and the like approved it. I say that because even though it was the Sabbath, they didn't shut down the pools, so they didn't disapprove it. This system was competitive and dangerous while not very fruitful at all.

This was not God's system. This was a folk belief *and* ritual tradition layered with Jewish superstition. Therefore: Jesus bypasses it entirely.

Bethesda is unique because it is the ONLY recorded place in the Bible where healing was competitive; like a game show. It was the "first come, first healed" idea, which made it fundamentally flawed. It **reflects man-made ritual rather than God-given Mercy.** It intentionally left most people disappointed. It produced fear, frustration, and helplessness and most likely pitted people against each other, before during and after the "stirring" of the water. God is not a God of disunity.

This is why Jesus bypassed the water entirely.

Bethesda is not just a miracle scene, it is a critique of every system that creates competition, breeds despair, confusion, elevates the strong over the weak, leaves people waiting for help that never comes. It is a system of favoritism in the sense that it lets one win while many lose.

Jesus *replaces* Bethesda with Himself.

In Scripture, Jesus healed all who came to Him. Scarcity was never from His hand. Whenever only one received, it was never because God lacked power, but because the moment carried Divine appointment, prophetic purpose, or a correction to a broken system. Bethesda is the clearest example not of God's limited Mercy, but of man's limited methods.

When you read that passage slowly, carefully and see that if God sent an angel to move the waters and only the first one who got in got healed, then Jesus coming by and healing others.... why would Jesus do something other than what God was doing? Further, where was this precedence in the Old Testament where God had an angel stationed somewhere who would sporadically come down and bless one person? Jesus came to fulfill the Law, after all.

This is when I began to ponder that the angel-at-the-water tradition at Bethesda was NOT commanded by God. The passage doesn't say God sent the angel. The angel is not named. Therefore, upon more study I found that this whole belief in this stirred water was a popular belief, not a Divine ordinance.

The earliest Greek manuscripts do NOT include the phrase about the angel stirring the water. The line: "For an angel went down at a certain season into the pool…" …was added *much later* by scribes trying to explain why people believed the water could heal. This means that it was a popular tradition, not a command from God. The pool's reputation was based on folk belief or legend.

Jesus did NOT contradict God and He never would and never will. Jesus did NOT contradict God by bypassing the water. Jesus corrected a broken human system, not a Divine one. **God never set up a "first one wins, the rest suffer" system. That's not His nature anywhere in Scripture.**

Bethesda was a mix of tradition, superstition, and Jewish healing custom. **God-ordained healing at Bethesda started when Jesus stepped onto that scene.** I am further clued in by the word **multitude** in the passage (John 5:3). Where there is a multitude, especially a mixt multitude that means there is a variety of people from various places with differing belief systems. A multitude is never one kind of person. It is a mixture of stories, beliefs, wounds, and hopes gathered in one place. Bethesda was a mosaic of humanity, and Jesus stepped into the middle of all of it. Folks could have been from all over. There were Jews there, for sure—it was Jerusalem. There were probably Samaritans, proselytes (non-Jews who followed Jewish customs), Greeks, Romans, travelers, sightseers, merchants, and those on pilgrimages from surrounding nations.

I do know that as I floated in the Dead Sea, I heard many languages from many different countries. Even the people in my touring group were from various cultures. Sickness and disease may be common to all, but how people seek to try to solve their problems can be very different.

The **multitude** at Bethesda was not a crowd of unified believers. It was a mix of cultures, conditions, and confusions. It was a picture of the world Jesus came to heal. Therefore, we don't judge them because we were called out of the multitude ourselves by Jesus Christ.

Scholars agree that Bethesda was known for its mineral springs. Some believed the bubbling meant an "angel *stirred* it. It became a healing shrine (like today's Lourdes or hot springs. People gathered because of rumor + desperation, not God's command.

The belief that it was healing may have grown from a natural spring eruption, a mineral reaction, a bubbling effect from an underground feeder, a coincidence of someone getting better. People associated the bubbling with an angel, but Scripture does *not* say God actually ordered it.

God's character NEVER aligns with "only the fastest get healed." Imagine if God truly set up a system like this: the strongest wins, the fastest wins, the most physically privileged wins, those with pretty privilege take the prize. The Gospels show in more than one instance that the rich man cannot buy his way into Heaven. The most superlative taking the prize is not God's system, any more than: the weak lose, the paralyzed have no chance, only one gets healed, and everyone else suffers. This contradicts the entire heart of God as revealed in the Books of the Law, the Prophets, the Psalms, the Gospels, and the entire ministry of Jesus. It is against the nature of Mercy. And we know that Grace is when we receive something good that we don't even deserve.

Nowhere else in Scripture does God make healing competitive or make it into a game. No where does He reward physical ability. He is not the author of the Olympic Games, (the polytheistic Greeks were.) Nowhere does God tie miracles to speed, or demand performance. He says the races is not to the swift. (Ecclesiastes 9:11) Solomon wrote that, and he was a man who believed in time and chance. We do not serve a God of "chance." His answers to our prayers are Yes, and Amen. Nowhere in Scriptures did God (or Jesus) heal only one person out of many or discriminate against the disabled.

As much as I wanted this book to be a lovely and graceful story about the wonders of Bethesda it has turned into a far greater Truth: that system at that pool was never God's idea. Jesus was spiritually confrontational. He came to set right what was wrong. He came to destroy the works of the devil. He came to seek and save those that were lost. Like the Old Testament prophets He came to heal the breach and build up the broken places. *If this was already a work of God that was working properly, why would Jesus even go there?*

When God sent plagues into Egypt, each plague was a smack-down to an idol *god* that Egyptians were serving. In the Gospels, Jesus goes places that are out of order to set things right. If there were idols being served at that pool, that could be why Jesus was there. God hates idolatry and we know that. *Right*?

Not only that, Bethesda Man got in trouble for carrying his bed on the Sabbath. Jesus allegedly got into all kinds of trouble in the Gospels for healing on the Sabbath. If that was to be an issue, then why were the people allowed around the Pool of Bethesda on the Sabbath? Is it because they didn't think the pool would really heal anyone, so it was okay for those people to gather or sit around the pool and waste their time? Pharisees had very strict rules about healing on the Sabbath. As said before, gathering, even lounging around that pool that was, had been, or was adjacent to idol temples was worship to those idol *gods*. Whether or not the people doing it, the person needing healing knew it or not. If you've got a mixed multitude they are coming for all kinds of reasons, not just for the God that we know and celebrate.

Jesus came to seek and save those who were lost. Jesus went out into the "streets" to places where people were doing the wrong thing to acquire something they needed. People either purposefully or mistakenly ask the wrong "*god*" for things all the time. It is the desperation or the pain or the fear of loss and great need that can drive man to desperate measures. Idolatry and idol *gods* rise when man gets desperate. This is why man must keep his faith in God and desire to only receive from God through Jesus Christ. This is why without faith it is impossible to please God.

Even if that thing they needed was a right thing, and it was healing. This is a picture of evangelism. Jesus, who ate with publicans and prostitutes, went to the lame, blind, halt, infirm and showed them Grace, and Mercy; He showed them God. And then they walked away from what was wrong, away from desperation and into what was godly, God's way, into what was Kingdom.

But Jesus

Jesus shows up to END the superstition around the Pool of Bethesda, not honor it. If the pool's system were truly God's, Jesus would have affirmed it. He would have helped Bethesda Man into the water. Jesus would have promoted this Pool and maybe even have sent people to it in some of His other ministry healings. As we know Jesus had the authority to call on angels, but there is no record that He did that at Bethesda.

Jesus had ultimate respect for the Father. He said, **"I only do what I see My Father do**." If God was sending an angel – an unknown angel to the pool to put enough power in it to heal only one person, then as a diligent Son, Jesus would have left that whole thing alone. If God sent you someplace and said that He was healing one person only in that place, would you then do whatever you want when you get there, as if God's plan needed tweaking?

Of course not.

So, instead of going along with the angel and the one-person-healed system, Jesus completely ignores the water. He ignores the ritual. He ignores superstition. Jesus is setting something right and we should suppose that it is unseen and we should look deeper. He ignores the competition and speaks to that man, to that man's spirit and tells him to **Rise**. He heals the man OUTSIDE the water system. And, Jesus heals Bethesda Man instantly, without waiting, without water, without an "angel."

Jesus is making a profound theological statement: Mercy does not operate by competition. Grace does not work for only one. Healing does not belong to the fast. (The first will be last, and the last will be first.) Jesus did not come to do away with the Law; He came to fulfill it. In doing this Jesus is saying, **"I am the fulfillment of Bethesda."**

which is his body, the fullness of him who fills everything in every way (Ephesians 1:23)

So why does the story include the tradition? Because the Bible records what people *believed*, not necessarily what God *commanded*. Just like "The Jews believed if you swore by the altar…" (Matt 23). "Some said John the Baptist had a demon…" but that did not make it true. "Some believed Elijah would return…" "The Pharisees said washing hands made you clean…" but Jesus was looking in their hearts. The Bible faithfully reports human beliefs even when those beliefs were wrong, incomplete, or distorted.

Bethesda is one of those moments. By discernment we are to rightly divide the Word and know Truth.

What Jesus did was not a contradiction; who of any of us would contradict God? And most of all, Jesus. It was a correction of man, his beliefs, and his system. You are not seeing God contradicting Himself; God is not a man that He should lie. Jesus came to fulfill the Law and not do away with it. Therefore, in this, you are seeing Jesus expose a system of belief. He rescued a man from his false beliefs – from his religion. Jesus bypassed and surpassed superstition. By showing more than enough Mercy and Grace for us all, Jesus ended competitive healing and showed us the heart of the Father.

Have you ever been in a healing service where one person gets called up and you never rise out of your seat, but there is enough anointing and power in that Word to heal all with faith to receive? I have. By the Holy Spirit you know when a Word is for you, and you can receive it and not have to race to the "pool" to get it. God can minister to us where we are, especially if we can't get to Him. Hallelujah & Amen.

That pool belief of the angel moving the water was a washing ritual, possibly legend and folklore. Lots of cultures believe and practice washing rituals, even today. Our Father is a God of relationship and Love, not ritual. Ritual is a function of obedience and obedience is how the Old Covenant functioned. Jesus showed Bethesda Man you don't have to risk your life or waste your life waiting if you are serving the One True God.

I'm not too bold to say these things because some of these "healing" pools that may have been nearby involved temples to idols, such as Fortuna.

Now, let's look deeper. If all those people are coming to this place day after day, staring at the water, waiting for it to move in some spiritual way, is this not worship? Sitting, attending to, paying attention to, staring at, hoping, wishing, expecting, and believing that something good was going to be given to (hopefully) you from this powerful pool or this powerful act or some powerful angel, is this not worship?

We will find out later that this pool was built either over, on, or adjacent to temples to idol *gods* and idol *gods* are very clever to get worship out of even unsuspecting people. How many people regularly trek to buy a lottery ticket knowing that usually only one person will win? This is religion; this is worship to the *idol god* over the lottery (and there is one). How many people enter a raffle for a brand-new car, and there is only one car; (same *god* as the lottery *god*)? This is worship, you put down your money, time, attention, belief and expectation in something that will bring you something, give you something, or help you in some way and that is religion, that is worship. If worship and faith is not towards Jehovah God, then it is by chance, and chance is idolatry.

By Jesus healing Bethesda Man, He ended this man's cycle of frustration, disadvantage, and abandonment. Jesus healed the man without the water, out of the water. Jesus bypassed the water, the competition, the system, the race, the ritual and all the previous rules that blocked a man from getting healed, for 38 years.

Jesus healed Bethesda Man *where he lay*. Jesus didn't just restore his body, He powerfully broke the spiritual cycle of almost," or "almost there." Jesus broke the cycle of the man sitting there staring at the water waiting for some hopeful *maybe*. Jesus broke idolatry off of Bethesda Man because Jesus healed him so he no longer thought that he needed the water to heal him, or that the water could heal him.

When Holy Water Isn't Holy: The Mixed History of Bethesda"

Archaeology reveals that the Pool of Bethesda was not a simple healing pool. Beneath St. Anne's Church in Jerusalem lie the remains of a complex that shifted in meaning over centuries, from a Jewish ritual bath, to a site associated with pagan healing practices, and eventually to a Christian church. Some scholars believe the pool may have been influenced at certain points by Greco-Roman healing cults — even possibly linked to shrines of Asclepius or Fortuna. These temples often used water as part of their rituals, promising healing to the first or the fortunate.

If this is true, then Jesus was doing more than healing one man. He was confronting a broken system, one that mixed superstition, competition, and spiritual confusion. A system where only the fastest, strongest, or luckiest received help.

Jesus did not honor the pool's reputation. He replaced it. His miracle made the water irrelevant.

Today, St. Anne's Church stands over the site as a testimony. Jesus heals where rituals fail, where superstition misleads, and where human systems exclude the weak. St. Anne's Church sits directly on top of the ancient remains of Bethesda.

So, in the past it was a Jewish *mikveh*, a place of ritual baths. Then came pagan influences and it became a healing place via cult patterns. After that, the Church redeemed it and Christians built a church over that site, St. Anne's Church. This literally shows God reclaiming the site. It is the same as an altar being captured by the enemy and then recaptured and rededicated to God, a pattern we have seen over and again in the Old Testament.

Grace + Water Is a Biblical Pattern

The combination of water and five flows throughout Scripture. There are five books of Moses which is the foundation for Covenant Grace. David carried five stones; reflecting Grace, which is a power. This power was great enough to overcome even giants. There were five loaves that fed thousands; this is Grace that multiplies. There are five offerings of Leviticus; this is Grace that atones, restores, and reconciles.

And the five wounds of Christ, which was Jesus Christ fulfilling all in all. That is Grace being poured out through the Body of Jesus.

So, when Jesus stands at a pool with five porches, healing a man who had no ability to help himself... ...it is a living demonstration of the Gospel. It is showing that Grace comes to you when you cannot reach the water or whatever *object* you have put belief into. Grace walks toward you when you cannot walk. Grace speaks life into you when your strength is gone.

Each pool in the Bible shows *something God does for us that we cannot do ourselves.* Each pool is an encounter where God's presence meets human limitation. Bethesda's five porches set the tone showing that healing begins with Grace. Every other pool then becomes a dimension of that Grace.

We review. Siloam is Grace that sends. Gibeon is Grace that confronts conflict, remembering that Grace is a power. Hezekiah's Pool is Grace that preserves; the water system for the city was moved so the enemy could not capture it. In addition, later there was more Grace: God added 15 years onto Hezekiah's life. Even desert pools are Grace that sustains in a dry and thirsty land where no water is, the Love of God is better than life. This is life-sustaining Grace.

The water of Baptism is Grace that transforms.

The water at the well is Living Water; it is Grace that saves us from eternal death.

In our world, there are many Bethesda's; there are many places called or named Bethesda. One in particular is Bethesda, Maryland, perhaps the most well-known Bethesda in the U.S. It is a major hub for medical research. NIH and Walter Reed Hospital are both there. It it a high-education, high-influence area with national reach and healing. This echoes what we have seen in Scriptures as Jesus healed the man that I call Bethesda Man.

In other states in the US, we find Bethesda, North Carolina, a community in Durham County. Bethesda, Arkansas a small community in Independence County. Bethesda, Wisconsin, a community in Dodge County. Bethesda Township, Ohio, Bethesda, West Virginia, a small community with early Methodist influence

In the UK, there is Bethesda, Gwynedd, Wales in Great Britain, a well-known Welsh village with strong historical spiritual roots, known for Welsh revivals. In Canada there is Bethesda, Ontario, a community north of Toronto, founded by settlers with strong Christian influence. In South Africa, we find Nieu-Bethesda. In Australia there is another Bethesda, and it is also associated with health and healing institutions (e.g., Bethesda Hospital)

If any of these other Bethesda's are named for the Bethesda in Jerusalem, it will be a place where Heaven meets human suffering. Bethesda should bring the message of hope, healing, Mercy, and restoration.

Prophetically a Bethesda could be where God brings healing to the world, through knowledge, compassion, and Mercy, so people aren't just sitting on their porches waiting for the water to stir, but instead letting the Love, Grace, and power of God stir in their hearts so they then look to Him for healing and not folk tales or legends. Bethesda's that are about healing must become infused with Christ, so people are not just sitting waiting and wasting time--, even years.

God's healing does not come through rituals. Throughout the Bible, God repeatedly interrupts human attempts to ritualize healing. Naaman wanted something dramatic; God gave him simple obedience. The Pool of Bethesda had a ritual system; Jesus bypassed it entirely. The Jordan River wasn't special—the obedience was. The Red Sea had no inherent power—God parted it. Even baptism is symbolic; God does the saving.

This is a truth repeated across Scripture. Healing flows from God's will, not human technique. Restoration comes from His presence, not formulas. Deliverance comes from Jesus, not steps or methods. Rituals without God are empty. Rituals with God are unnecessary. God Himself is the power behind every healing in Scripture.

For those who are seeking healing, you don't have to go to Bethesda Israel, or Bethesda – anywhere, unless God says so. Even if you are on a bed of affliction, Jesus can meet you there. Listen closely as He says, **"Rise, take up your bed and walk."** Your spirit man will hear. That power will be infused into your spirit man and it must obey the Spirit of God.

Be healed. Be made whole. Amen.

The Symbolism of "38 Years"

The man at Bethesda had been in that condition for 38 years. That number is not random; it echoes a major biblical pattern. 38 Years = Israel's Wandering in the Wilderness (Deuteronomy 2:14). This is the most direct and widely recognized biblical link. Israel wandered 38 years from the time they left Kadesh-barnea until they crossed into a new season.

Not 40 — the total was 40 but *38 years* passed after the moment they refused to enter the Promised Land.

So, 38 symbolizes a long season of frustration—in the Wilderness. It is said that the walk to the Promised Land should have taken 11 days. They got stuck in a cycle that should have ended earlier. Constant delays, stagnation and being stuck on "repeat," waiting for breakthrough that seems overdue. Or stuck in a state of spiritual paralysis with promises unfulfilled--, life on pause.

This perfectly describes Bethesda Man. He wasn't just sick; he was stuck.

By God and because of God, through Jesus , the Christ of God, Bethesda becomes the place where cycles break, and delay ends.

38 equals the end of human ability, the limit of self-effort. The man said, "I have no one to help me." 38 years symbolizes the point at which human help has failed, self-effort is exhausted. By then, systems have let you down and you've realized that your own strength cannot deliver you. You cannot move any further, any closer. Even though you are looking righ at it, you cannot "get yourself into the water."

Jesus shows up at the end of human possibility. In Biblical symbolism, 38 represents human inability meeting Divine Mercy.

38 = Incomplete Deliverance (40 = completion) In Scripture, 40 = fullness, completion, transition whereas 38 is *not quite there.*

For the flood, God sent 40 days and nights of rain. Moses spent 40 days on Sinai. Jesus was in the Wilderness for 40 days and the Israelites were in their Wilderness state for 40 years.

So, 38 represents "almost." It indicates an unfulfilled promise, an unfinished journey, and the threshold before breakthrough, the moment right before transition. This is the emotional and spiritual condition of Bethesda Man. He is one step away from completion, but he cannot finish it himself.

Only Jesus can.

38 is the moment before divine intervention.

In Hebrew thinking, numbers also tell stories; therefore, 38 symbolizes the moment right before change, the long wait before the turning point, and the build-up before transformation. It is the number of not yet, the number of hanging between seasons, the number of waiting for the Word to be spoken.

People stand at their own pools, in long seasons of "not yet," waiting for God to speak into their story.

The number 38 carries a depth of meaning woven through Scripture. It marks the end of human strength, the exhaustion of self-effort, and the long seasons where breakthrough feels just out of reach. Both Israel in the wilderness and Bethesda Man lived under this number—stuck, delayed, unable to move forward without Divine intervention.

Thirty-eight is the number of long waiting. In Deuteronomy 2:14, Israel wandered 38 years after refusing to enter the Promised Land. It was a season of delay, frustration, paralysis, cycles that would not break, dreams deferred, and unfulfilled potential.

Likewise, Bethesda Man lived 38 years in his condition. His story mirrors Israel's inability to rise, enter, move forward, and enter in. He had to watch others step in while he remained stuck. Both represent the human condition apart from Divine help.

Thirty- Nine (39) -- Between Delay & Destiny

So, let's talk about 39; it is the bridge between human limitation and Divine healing. Paul reminds us that *"by His stripes we are healed."* Tradition holds that Jesus received **39 lashes. He received** forty minus one, which represents the fullness of suffering before death.

Spiritually and numerically, 39 stands between:

- **38** (incomplete, stuck) and

- **40** (completion.

Jesus becomes the bridge between what we cannot change and what only God can complete. **40 — The Number of Completion and New Beginnings**

Forty marks the moment of transition. Israel entered the Promised Land after 40 years. Jesus began His ministry after 40 days. Elijah journeyed 40 days on supernatural strength.

Forty represents new chapters, promises fulfilled, the end of wandering and the beginning of purpose

The Spiritual Pattern: 38 → 39 → 40, seen together, these numbers tell a powerful story:

- **38** — Human limitation, stuckness, long waiting.

- **39** — Jesus' suffering, healing, and intervention.

- **40** — Breakthrough, transition, new beginnings.

Jesus steps into the place where human ability ends. He breaks the cycle that cannot be broken alone. He completes what we cannot complete. He carries us from paralysis to purpose.

His stripes stand between your long waiting and your new beginning.

So many people come to the water to look, but sometimes God is saying to get in, step in. Moses and then Joshua had to step in. Have you noticed how many people flock to beaches to sunbathe, but far fewer of them actually get in the water. They just want to BE there. Many people who go to beaches cannot even swim; they just want to BE there. Some of them are just looking at the water, because most often it is beautiful. Some are there to listen to the waves roll in; that rhythmic sound can be very soothing.

As Christians we worship God only and not His Creation which includes the water, the beaches, the sun – anything God has created. Amen.

Human parents, we all know that full-term gestation in pregnancy is 40 weeks. That again speaks of fullness and completion. As easy or as difficult as it may be, no mother-to-be would refuse divine help in pregnancy and especially at delivery. Let the Spirit of God, let the angel of the Lord assist every delivery of every new life coming to Earth, in the Name of Jesus. As the count down goes from 38 weeks to 39, to 40— Thank You, Lord. Amen.

Reflection Questions:

In what area or areas of your life do you feel like you're at 38 and possibly stuck?

In what areas or areas of your life do you need Jesus right now and His 39 to bridge you into the promises of God?

_____

_____

_____

_____

_____

Celebrate the Lord in areas where He has fully delivered you. They overcame by the Blood of the Lamb and by the word of their testimony.

_____

_____

_____

_____

_____

_____

_____

_____

_____

Your Pool — Where God Meets You Today

Every pool in Scripture carries a universal message, but each one also speaks personally. Bethesda reveals Mercy. Siloam: obedience. Gibeon: conflict. The King's Pool: awareness. Hezekiah's Pool: preparation. Desert pools: provision. Baptismal waters: new creation. All of these lead to one final truth: God desires to meet you at your own pool—right where you are.

This chapter is an invitation to recognize the sacredness of your present moment. You may not be standing beside an ancient spring or walking the stone pathways of Jerusalem, but the same God who moved in those places moves in your life today. The waters of Scripture become mirrors, reflecting how God engages your heart, your struggles, your healing, and your destiny.

Identifying Your Pool

Your pool may look different depending on the season of life you are in:

- **Bethesda**: Are you waiting for Mercy? Holding onto hope after years of disappointment? Feeling overlooked or forgotten?

_____

_____

_____

_____

_____

_____

_____

_____

_____

_____

_____

_____

_____

_____

- **Siloam**: Is God calling you to step out in obedience, even before you see the outcome? Are you walking your miracle out by faith?

_____

_____

_____

_____

_____

_____

_____

_____

_____

_____

_____

- **Gibeon**: Are you facing conflict, unresolved tension, or internal battles that reveal deeper truths about your heart?

- **The King's Pool**: Is God asking you to confront brokenness with honesty and courage, inviting you to see what must be rebuilt?

- **Hezekiah's Pool:** Are you in a season of preparation, where God is strengthening what lies beneath the surface?

_____

_____

_____

_____

_____

_____

_____

- **Desert Pools:** Are you wandering through a dry place, seeking refreshment, clarity, or a hidden well of provision?

_____

_____

_____

_____

_____

_____

Baptismal Waters: Are you being called into renewal, rebirth, or a fresh identity in Christ?

_____

_____

_____

_____

_____

_____

_____

_____

_____

_____

_____

Your journey may pass through many of these waters. Each one reveals a facet of God's heart and a pathway toward deeper healing.

God Meets You in the Ordinary

Not every pool in Scripture was a dramatic scene of miracles. Some were quiet, hidden, or easily overlooked. In the same way, God often meets us in ordinary places, such as in conversations. He definitely can meet us in moments of stillness. We find

Him and He locates us through Scripture, during prayer and during worship.

God can locate us in the midst of daily routines.

Your pool may be a place of prayer, a moment of surrender, a renewed promise, or a gentle whisper from the Holy Spirit.

Bringing Your Brokenness to God

The invitation of this chapter—and of this entire journey—is simple: bring your whole self to the waters or appointed places of healing. Bring your fears, your hopes, your questions, your wounds, your dreams. God specializes in meeting people in vulnerable places. He does not avoid brokenness; He enters it.

Just as Jesus approached the man at Bethesda, God draws near to you. He sees your story. He knows the places where you long for healing. And He comes not with condemnation, but with compassion.

The Waters That Stir Within You

This book has traced the physical pools of Scripture, but the true waters God cares about are the ones within your soul. Jesus spoke of "living water"—

a spring that rises from within, flowing eternal life, healing, and transformation (John 7:38).

These inner waters are stirred by the Word of God, the presence of the Holy Spirit, times in praise and worship, acts of obedience, encounters with God's Love, even in divine dreams and in seasons of repentance and renewal.

Your pool is not simply a location; it is a meeting place between your heart and God's presence.

Stepping Into Your Waters

No matter which pool your life currently reflects, God is inviting you to step into the waters. Rise out of places where you felt stuck. Wash yourself in obedience to His Word. Truthfully confront what must be healed. Embrace preparation and resilience. Receive and drink deeply of His provision. Enter into the newness of life.

The same God who moved in ancient Israel moves in the landscape of your heart. The waters are stirred. The invitation has been given.

Come to the pool. God is waiting for you there.

Reflection Questions:

1. **Which biblical pool reflects your current spiritual season?**

_____

_____

_____

_____

_____

_____

_____

_____

2. **What step of faith is God inviting you to take at your own pool?**

_____

_____

_____

_____

_____

The Power of the Waters — Above and Below

From the very first verses of Scripture, water is revealed not as a passive element but as a **power,** a force ordered, divided, and assigned by God for Divine purpose. Before land, before light, before time itself was counted, there were waters above and waters below, separated by the Word of God.

This division is not only cosmological; it is theological. It sets the stage for how water functions throughout the entire biblical narrative. In my book, **Powers Above & Powers Below** that revelation now connects seamlessly to the theme of this book. The healing pools of Scripture are part of a much larger movement. The waters are powers that God ordained from the beginning.

The Waters Above and the Waters Below

Genesis tells us: *"And God separated the waters which were under the expanse from the waters which were above the expanse.* " (Genesis 1:7). These waters represent two realms:

- The waters above — the realm of the heavens, the unseen, the spiritual.

- The waters below — the realm of the Earth, the visible, the physical.

All the waters in Scripture—every river, every sea, every well, every pool flows from this original division. They carry meaning, power, and purpose far beyond geography.

Symbol Glossary

Water

Represents life, cleansing, renewal, the Holy Spirit, and God's active presence. It symbolizes both Creation and recreation, judgment and, chaos and order, death and rebirth.

Pools

Symbolic places of encounter where God meets human need. Pools represent waiting, healing, reflection, transition, and divine timing.

Wells

Symbols of provision, revelation, and sustenance. Wells represent Divine insight, spiritual depth, and encounters with God in hidden or unexpected places.

Rivers

Signs of movement, power, and the unstoppable flow of God's Spirit. Rivers symbolize life, direction, transformation, and the ongoing work of God.

Springs

Symbols of freshness, renewal, and God's ability to bring life from dry places. Springs represent hope, revival, and the emergence of new beginnings.

Water as a Divine Instrument

In review, throughout Scripture, water becomes the medium through which God Creates, (as seen in Genesis 1), God Judges by the Flood. He delivers by parting the Red Sea. He Sanctifies by water. God first ordained ritual washings; others copied or distorted them. He heals by water; He healed Naaman through the prophet. He healed at Bethesda and also Siloam through His Christ. God commissions via water Baptism. Water speaks: (the voice of many waters). God also through water, reveals as in Ezekiel's temple river.

Water holds Divine authority because God assigned it purpose at Creation.

The Power of Water in Healing

In the healing narratives, water is more than background. It carries cleansing power, washing away impurity. Water has transformative power, shifting identity through Baptism. It has transitional power, marking the passage from old to new. Water has obedience power; where the miracle is unlocked by action (Moses stretching his staff, Joshua stepping into the Jordan, Naaman dipping seven times).

And it has reflective power — mirroring the soul's condition.

People came to the waters to observe, admire, or wait—but God often called His people to enter into the water. Water was not entered into nor applied at Bethesda; that was all Jesus.

Looking at the Water vs. Entering Its Power

Many gather near the water's edge, but only a few step in. On beaches today, crowds flock to the shoreline to sunbathe, relax, and dwell near the water's beauty—but far fewer enter the water itself. They want proximity without immersion.

The same is true spiritually. At the Red Sea, Israel stood before the water in fear until Moses lifted his hand. At the Jordan, Israel stood on the banks until the priests placed their feet in. At Bethesda, multitudes waited near the pool, but one man was healed because the Living Water approached him.

God often requires movement—not just presence.

Water as Boundary and Gateway

Biblical water always marks a boundary. From Egypt it demarcated slavery from freedom. Led by Moses and then Joshua, that water separated the Wilderness from the Promise. In Baptism it is the line between Death and resurrection--, newness of life.

But that very same boundary becomes a gateway when God speaks. Water can divide, but since it is God's creation, God can divide the waters.

The Waters

The healing pools of Scripture have been looked at very closely in this volume. When people come to the edge of these waters, some will admire, some will wait, but the ones who step in will encounter God. But we have learned from Jesus, that is not the only way to experience the Love, Mercy, Grace, and power of God. Jesus came right up to Bethesda Man. Jesus will locate you just where you are, especially if you pray. Especially if you ask Him, "Lord, look on me." "I am in need." I am stuck." "Stuck at 38 – stuck at 38 years, days, weeks, 38 months. "I need You, Lord."

This chapter invites you, Dear Reader to move from observation to immersion, from distance to participation, from looking at the water to entering its power.

Reflection Questions:

1. **How do you see the waters of Scripture at work in your own story?**

---

2. **Are you standing at the edge, observing, or stepping into the power God has offered?**

Gentle Redirect for Practice-Mixers

A Note to Readers from Mixed Spiritual Backgrounds:

Many of us have explored spiritual practices—some from childhood tradition, some from curiosity, some from the internet, and some simply because we were searching for peace. You may have tried crystals, sage, protective baths, moon phases, or energy cleansing without ever considering them "spiritual practices." You may have simply wanted calm, clarity, or comfort.

Some may have tried heavier rituals or may have even been born into them, or forced by parents into things that are not of God or from God. It is by the Truth of the Word of God and the Holy Spirit that you will know if you have stepped out of alignment with God.

This book is written with you in mind—not to condemn you, but to recenter you. Biblical healing does not require you to create an atmosphere or harness energy. It does not require you to activate a ritual, or perform rituals. It does not require that you give blood or harm yourself or others. It does not require that you "cleanse your aura," invoke elements, use herbs or crystals, chant, or time your healing to the moon. God does not ask you to cleanse yourself in order to come to Him. He cleanses you when you do.

If you have used other spiritual tools, know this: You are loved. You are welcome. God is not holding anything against you. He does not desire that one soul be lost to the dark or any false "kingdom." And you do not need those tools to be safe, protected, or spiritually whole.

The God of Scripture does not require enhancements, elements, objects, charms, or rituals. He only asks for you. Let this book return you gently to the Truth.

The water in and of itself cannot cleanse you. Moon water cannot cleanse you. The ritual cannot heal you—well, not permanently. The crystal cannot protect you. Only Jesus can.

There is no need for covetousness, competition or greed; there is plenty good room in the Kingdom of God. God's Grace and anointing is more than enough for all. God does not have children that He can't or won't take care of.

That only one got "healed" at Bethesda each season was an indication that this was NOT God's ultimate desire — it was a picture of how insufficient human systems are without Christ. Now this is just a question, but whether you got healed by the "water" at Bethesda or not, wouldn't the average person be tempted to come back every season and rush into the water when it "moved" to KEEP FROM GETTING SICK, or getting sick again, or getting sick, ever? This is only human nature. So, what chance would a person who is really sick have of getting in that water?

Jesus Became Our Bethesda

Bethesda was a place of Mercy, but it was limited – to one. It was limited to the first one in the pool after the moving of the waters. It was a place of competition and striving as the race was given to the first one to and into the pool. And for those who weren't first, it was a place of disappointment. Jesus comes to END that system.

This is why He healed Bethesda Man without using the water. As beautiful as the Pool of Bethesda is depicted, it was a place of many dangers, which we have discussed. Jesus didn't just heal that man's life; he saved it. Jesus healed the man outside of the pool intentionally, to show that Grace doesn't work like scarcity. It is Him saying, **"My Mercy is not for the first — it is for *all*."**

This is reminiscent of the Parable of the Penny when those who came in first were upset with those who came in later or last but they all made the same— a penny. That is the nature of God. So, no matter your age, even if you are 40, 50, or 100 years old, it is not too late to accept Christ as Your Lord and Savior. You are welcomed and you will receive the same Love, the same Mercy, the same Grace as the one who came to Christ as a child or teen. THAT is the system and the Love of God. It reveals the difference between Law and Grace.

Bethesda, before Jesus, was a law-based system, but Jesus didn't come to do away with the Law, but to fulfill it. Law brings order, Grace brings Mercy and favor. In the law-based system, only one is healed and only at a certain time, only under certain conditions, only with the right response. This mirrors the old covenant reality that blessings depended on timing and obedience, sacrifices depended on procedure, access to God depended on rituals, and atonement depended on the priest.

Grace changes everything. Bethesda becomes the bridge between the old and the new. When Jesus shows up, healing is personal, abundant, immediate, not earned, not limited, not competitive.

Jesus *supersedes* the scarcity model.

It exposes the inability of human strength. Only the first could get in. Who gets there first? The strong; those not as sick. The fast, those not debilitated. The connected; the ones with helpers. The ones who already have advantage. So, God allowed a system that revealed human inequality, not to endorse it, but so that Jesus could overturn it. The man Jesus healed had no one to help him. He probably was the least likely to ever reach the water.

Therefore: God waited for the one who had *zero chance* to demonstrate that healing is not about human strength at all. It showed that he who probably would have been last, became first. Amen.

It teaches that the place was not the source — God was. People believed that the water healed, that the angel healed, that the stirring healed. But Jesus shows: No. The water was only a signpost. God is the Healer. The water is not the power — Jesus is.

This is similar to Moses lifting the bronze serpent; healing wasn't in the statue. The Jordan River; healing wasn't in the water, it was by the Spirit of God. The hem of Jesus' garment; power wasn't in the fabric or the tassels from the garment. God uses means, but the means are not the power.

However — the Bethesda limitation wasn't about God loving "first" people more. It was about pointing toward something better.

The water healed only one, so that Jesus could heal all.

Jesus replaced Bethesda. Jesus didn't wait for the water. He *didn't* help the man into the pool. He *didn't* wait for an angel to stir anything.

He said, "**Rise.**"

The limitations of the pool system ended that day. That day, Bethesda becomes a picture of Old Covenant: limited Mercy versus New Covenant Jesus and unlimited Grace. The "first one in" model ended when Love Himself walked in.

In summary, the reason only the first was healed was to show the inadequacy of the old system. The scarcity of pre-Christ healing, the failure of human strength, the difference between law and Grace. The necessity of Jesus. The power of discernment. The shift from ritual to relationship.

Jesus *becomes* our Bethesda. Just as Rehoboth became Isaac's place of room, space, and flourishing... Jesus becomes the place where we are healed, restored, and made whole. Jesus is the appointed place of our healing.

By His stripes, we were healed. Jesus is an appointed place of healing.

And the LORD said, Behold, *there is* a place by me, and thou shalt stand upon a rock (Exodus 33:12)

In Genesis, with Isaac, we see that Rehoboth means, enlargement, freedom. Genesis 26 shows Isaac digging wells that were contended for--, *Esek* means disputed, fought over. *Sitnah* means, hostility. closed to him (blocked by Philistines). But the well he finally dug was uncontested. Rehoboth, meaning *the LORD has made room for us*. It was the place where the striving ended. Contention ceased. Isaac could now breathe and flourish. He could now settle without opposition and he had space to grow.

Rehoboth was the place of peace after conflict.

Bethesda by name was a "House of Mercy" But a Mercy limited by the old system… until Jesus. Before Jesus, Bethesda was a place of waiting, a place of frustration, a place of competition, a place of scarcity, a place of disappointment. A place of either low power or low compassion, or both; only one would be healed. It was a dangerous place. Just as lottery winners may brag when they win, they seldom say how many times or how much they've lost trying to "win." If the Pool of Bethesda was set over or adjacent to temples dedicated to idol *gods*, how much did the infirm people their lose in hopes of gaining their health, strength and mobility? Besides physical danger, there was also spiritual danger there.

How many of them dove into the pool and didn't get healed or come out alive? Those were sacrifices to those idols. How many were initiated or indoctrinated just by being there day after day? Let these words caution the reader that idols are very sneaky to get worship and to initiate people even when they don't think they are doing anything wrong.

So, pray very well that you haven't inadvertently joined into any idolatry and that you aren't mistakenly worshipping any idols. Stay prayed up so that neither you nor your family are candidates for any evil. Pray very well that you never enter desperation. Know very well that you receive blessings and gifts only from God through the Lord Jesus Christ. This way you aren't roped into any strange religion. Amen.

So, in that system, only one got the prize while Everyone else remained broken. These are things you can look for to discern if a thing, a system is of God or not. A third part of the stars (angels) defected with Lucifer when he fell from Heaven. Every "angel" is not God's angel, therefore we must be very wise, discerning, and prayerful.

When Jesus walked in, He *did not* work within that system. He *replaced* it. He overruled it entirely. He became the new source of healing. Not the water. Not the angel. Not the timing. Himself.

Isaac's Rehoboth was his room to flourish. When Jesus came this led to our room to heal. Rehoboth ended Isaac's striving for provision. Bethesda ends our striving for healing. Isaac said, "God has made room for us.

Jesus says, **"Rise. Walk. Come to Me. There is room in My Mercy."** Bethesda's water healed one. Jesus heals all who come to Him. Bethesda demanded competition. Jesus brings compassion. Bethesda required the afflicted to get in. Jesus goes *to* the afflicted.

Bethesda offered Grace for one. Jesus *is* limitless, abundant Grace.

Jesus is not just "at" the Pool — He *becomes* the Pool. The water that healed one man was replaced by the Living Water that heals all. Jesus becomes our Rehoboth, a place of space and flourishing. Our Bethesda, our place of Mercy and healing. Our Siloam (place of sending). Jordan is a place of crossing and transition. Jesus is our well in the wilderness, the Rock that waters. Our spring in drought. He is our river of living water.

He becomes every pool we need. As Rehoboth became Isaac's place of room, Jesus becomes our Bethesda —, our place of healing, Mercy, and restoration. Where Isaac found space in Rehoboth, we find healing in Jesus, our Bethesda.

Rehoboth ended Isaac's striving. Bethesda ends ours — because Jesus is both.

The Waters Are Stirred

Across the pages of Scripture, the waters rise, fall, part, flow, heal, and speak. From the waters of Creation to the waters of baptism, from the pools of Jerusalem to the hidden wells in the wilderness, water has always been the place where God meets humanity. These waters reveal His character, His Mercy, His power, His patience, and His desire to restore what has been broken.

Each pool in this book represents a moment of divine interruption. Bethesda — where Mercy finds the forgotten. Siloam — where obedience unlocks purpose. Gibeon — where conflict exposes the heart. The King's Pool — where truth prepares the way for rebuilding. Hezekiah's Pool — where preparation protects the future. Desert Pools — where God sustains in barren places. Baptismal Waters — where new life begins. And even the breaking of the mother's water, so a new life can be born on Earth.

Your Pool — where God meets you today.

And remember, the Powers of the Waters — where Heaven touches Earth.

This journey through the waters reveals one truth above all: God is neither distant nor silent. He is present at every pool. In waiting seasons, in wilderness places, in moments of conflict, and on the threshold of new beginnings—He is there. The waters of Scripture teach us how God moves, how He heals, and how He invites us to step into the story He is writing in our lives.

The waters are stirred, and the invitation is given. Wherever you stand—by Bethesda's porches, Siloam's path, Gibeon's edge, or the wilderness spring—may you have the courage to step in, the faith to obey, and the heart to receive the healing that flows from God's appointed places. If you cannot get to the water, if you cannot get to God, ask Him earnestly to meet you right where you are. Jesus does not avoid the blind, deaf, lame, or disabled. He will come right where you are and if you have faith, He will minister to you right there, even if it is a bed of affliction, torment, emotional pain or shame. He is not holding anything against you, no matter what the enemy has told you. Jesus desires that not one is lost. He wants you saved. Amen.

From Broken Pools to Redeemed Places — The Witness of St. Anne's Church

When you stand today at the Pool of Bethesda, you do not stand beside a shrine to competition, superstition, or ritual. You do not stand in the shadow of a system that healed one and abandoned many. Instead, rising over the ancient stones and the fractured pools is St. Anne's Church, a quiet and reverent place built by followers of Christ centuries after Jesus walked through those porches.

It is not by accident that a Christian church rests on top of a site once tangled in layers of folk belief, ritual attempts, and—if some historians are correct—even pagan healing practices. What once represented confusion now carries clarity. What once held desperation now holds worship. What once whispered of a healing that could never keep its promises now proclaims the name of the One who keeps every promise He makes.

St. Anne's Church is more than architecture. It is a proclamation in stone.

Jesus redeems places. Jesus reclaims stories. Jesus restores sites of failure and turns them into testimonies. The man at Bethesda was healed without touching the water. The pool itself was healed without needing a miracle. Because when Jesus steps into a place, the place becomes a sanctuary.

St. Anne's is the final echo of the story: Bethesda failed; Jesus didn't and Jesus doesn't. The Pool of Bethesda was not a good or Godly system, but Mercy won the day and Bethesda Man was healed. Jesus can heal whosoever will; He died for all of us. At Bethesda, the system collapsed, but the Savior stood. Bethesda Man stood and he also walked. The waters in the pool may or may not have stirred, but Jesus, the Word spoke and stirred Bethesda Man's faith and his spirit. He arose and was healed.

When Mercy and Grace speak, we all are embraced in Love, and Truth, then Peace, Health, Healing and Joy can be ours. Salvation and eternal life can be ours.

And the Word is still speaking. Are you listening?

Epilogue

To visit Bethesda today is to walk downward—descending through time layer by layer. The sun falls across broken stone steps, cracked arches, and the deep-cut outlines of the two great pools. The air inside the ruins is cool, almost still. You can trace the five porticos with your eyes, imagining the rows of the sick who once gathered in the shadows.

Above you, the soft Romanesque arches of St. Anne's Church rise in quiet majesty. Its pale stones glow in the light, and when you step inside, a holy hush wraps around you. The acoustics of the sanctuary make even a whisper sound like a psalm. Pilgrims sing hymns there—not loudly, but with the reverence of those who know they are standing where God rewrote a story.

Looking down at the pools from the edge of the church courtyard, you can almost feel the contrast: the ruins below whispering of human attempts at healing… the church above testifying of divine Grace that succeeded where systems failed.

Bethesda is no longer a place of waiting. It is a place of remembrance. A place where Jesus

walked, healed, confronted, restored, and redeemed—
then left a witness in stone to say:

"This is what I do with broken places."

Blessing — A Prayer Over Your Waters

A Closing Blessing

May the waters of Scripture awaken something
deep within you—
not the waters that move by chance,
nor the waters stirred by fear or superstition,
but the waters touched by the presence of Jesus.

May you find Him not only beside the pools of
your life,
but standing within them,
turning every place of disappointment
into a fountain of unexpected Grace.

May every forgotten corner of your heart
echo with the Mercy and Love of Jesus Christ.

May every season of waiting
become an invitation to encounter Him anew.
And may every broken place in your story
rise beneath His touch—
as the restored man rose,
carrying the bed that once carried him.

May the Lord bless you with living water—
water that heals what hurt you,
water that restores what was taken,
water that remembers what you tried to forget,

water that runs from eternity
and returns you to Peace.

Go now in the Grace of the One who sees you,
the One who meets you,
the One who heals without ritual
and restores without delay.

And may you find Him—
again and again—
at every appointed place of Mercy.

Amen.

If you had only known what kind of water I have…. (Jesus)

AMEN.

Sinner's Prayer for Salvation

Lord, have Mercy on me, a sinner. Give me a Godly sorrow for my sin and a repentant heart. Lord hear my repentance and if I am none of Yours, make me one of Yours.

I believe that Jesus is the Son of God and that He came to Earth and died, but on the Third Day God resurrected Him and He lives.

I believe in my heart and I confess with my mouth that Jesus is Lord. Come into my heart and be the Lord of my life.

I am now saved.

Thank You, Lord

In Jesus' Name,

Amen.

Scriptures for Healing

Old Testament

- Exodus 15:26 — *"I am the Lord who heals you."*

- Psalm 30:2 — *"O Lord my God, I cried to You for help, and You healed me."*

- Psalm 103:2–3 — *He forgives all your sins and heals all your diseases.*

- Proverbs 4:20–22 — *His words are life and health to the whole body.*

- Isaiah 53:5 — *By His stripes we are healed.*

- Jeremiah 17:14 — *Heal me, O Lord, and I shall be healed.*

Gospels

- Matthew 4:23 — Jesus healed every disease and sickness among the people.

- Matthew 8:16–17 — *He took our infirmities and bore our diseases.*

- Mark 5:34 — *"Daughter, your faith has made you well."*

- Mark 10:52 — *"Go your way; your faith has made you well."*

- Luke 4:18 — *He has anointed Me to heal the brokenhearted.*

- John 5:8–9 — *"Rise, take up your bed, and walk."*

Acts & Epistles

- Acts 10:38 — Jesus went about doing good and healing all.

- Romans 8:11 — The Spirit gives life to your mortal body.

- 1 Corinthians 12:9 — Gifts of healing by the same Spirit.

- James 5:14–15 — Prayer of faith will save the sick.

- 1 Peter 2:24 — *By His wounds you were healed.

Dear Reader

Thank you for acquiring, reading, and sharing this book.

Blessings and Divine health to you, in the Name of Jesus,

Amen.

Dr. Marlene Miles

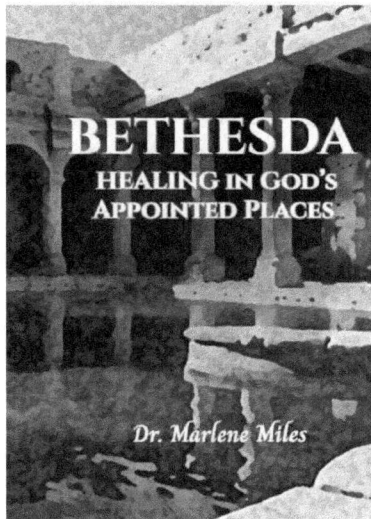

Father: I seal this work, this word, these prayers, decrees, and declarations from now to infinity against in every dimension, timeline and age, past present and future. I seal it with the Holy Spirit of Promise and the Blood of Jesus. Any retaliation against the author, reader or anyone using any part of this book at any time in the future, backfire against the perpetrator, in the Name of Jesus. Amen.

Prayer Books by this Author
Prayer Manuals

FAKE FRIENDS: *Prayers Against Betrayers*

HOLIDAY WARFARE Prayer Manual (humorous) Surviving Family Gatherings All Year Long (without catching a case)

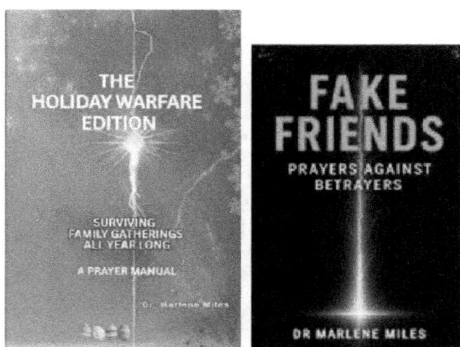

SOUL TIE Prayer Manual (The) Part of a 3-part series including a workbook.

MAD at DADDY Prayer Manual – part of a 3-part series including a workbook.

Healing the Sibling & Relative Wound Prayer Manual

Healing the Father-Son Wound Prayer Manual

Prayers Against Barrenness: *For Success in Business and Life*

Breaking My Mother's (unintentional) Curses Prayer Manual

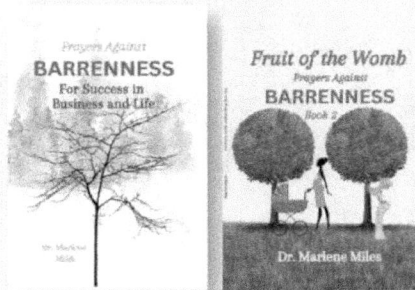

Prayers Against Barrenness: *For Success in Business and Life*

Fruit of the Womb: *Prayers Against Barrenness*

Beauty Curses, *Warfare Prayers Against*
https://a.co/d/5Xlc20M

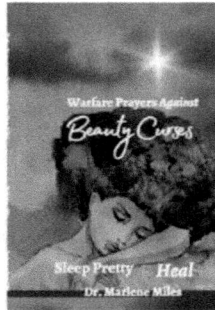

Courts of Marriage: Prayers for Marriage in the Courts of Heaven *(prayerbook)* https://a.co/d/cNAdgAq

Courtroom Warfare @ Midnight *(prayerbook)*
https://a.co/d/5fc7Qdp

Demonic Cobwebs *(prayerbook)* https://a.co/d/fp9Oa2H

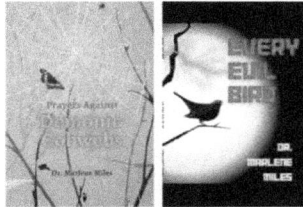

Every Evil Bird https://a.co/d/hF1kh1O

Every Evil Arrow https://a.co/d/afgRkiA

Gates of Thanksgiving

Spirits of Death & the Grave, Pass Over Me and My House https://a.co/d/dS4ewyr

*Please note that my name is spelled incorrectly on amazon, but not on the book.

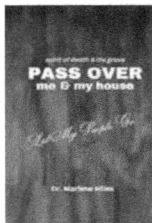

Throne of Grace: Courtroom Prayer

https://a.co/d/fNMxcM9

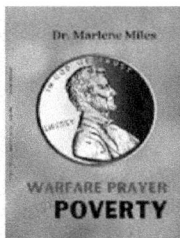

Warfare Prayer Against Poverty
https://a.co/d/bZ611Yu

Other books by this author

AK: *The Adventures of the Agape Kid*

AMONG SOME THIEVES

Ancestral Powers https://a.co/d/9prTyFf

ANTI-KAREN: *How To Mind Your Own Business Without Minding Other People's*

Backstabbers https://a.co/d/gi8iBxf

Barrenness, *Prayers Against* https://a.co/d/feUltIs

Battlefield of Marriage, *The*

BETHESDA: Healing In God's Appointed Places

Blindsided: *Has the Old Man Bewitched You?* https://a.co/d/5O2fLLR

Break Free from Collective Captivity

Breaking the (unintentional) Curses of My Mother

Casting Down Imaginations https://a.co/d/1UxlLqa

Churchcraft: Witchcraft In the Church

Churchzilla, The Wanna-Be, Supposed-to-be Bride of Christ

Curses of Blind Men

Demonic Cobwebs (prayerbook)

Demonic Time Bombs

Demons Hate Questions

Devil Loves Trauma, *The*

Devil Weapons: Unforgiveness, Bitterness,...

The Devourers: *Thieves of Darkness 2*

Do Not Swear by the Moon

Don't Refuse Me, Lord (4 book series)

https://a.co/d/idP34LG

Dream Defilement

The Emptiers: *Thieves of Darkness, 1*
https://a.co/d/5I4n5mc

ENTANGLEMENTS: *Illegal Knots Limiting Your Life*

Every Evil Arrow https://a.co/d/afgRkiA

Evil Touch https://a.co/d/gSGGpS1

Failed Assignment https://a.co/d/3CXtjZY

Fantasy Spirit Spouse https://a.co/d/hW7oYbX

FAT Demons (The): *Breaking Demonic Curses*

The Fold (5-book series)

- The Fold (Book 1)
- Name Your Seed (Book 2)
- The Poor Attitudes of Money (3)
- Do Not Orphan Your Seed (4)
- For the Sake of the Gospel (5)
- My Sowing Journal

Gang Ups: *Touch Not God's Anointed*

got HEALING? Verses for Life

got LOVE? Verses for Life

got HOPE? Verses for Life

got money? https://a.co/d/g2av41N

How to Dental Assist

How to Dental Assist2: Be Productive, Not Wasteful

How To Stay Prayed Up

I Take It Back

Legacy

Let Me Have A Dollar's Worth https://a.co/d/h8F8XgE

Level the Playing Field

Living for the NOW of God

Lose My Location https://a.co/d/crD6mV9

Mad At Daddy (3 book series)

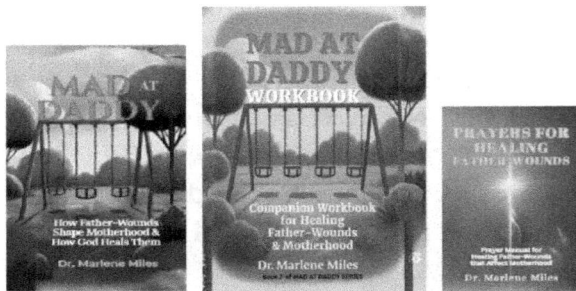

MAD AT DADDY: *How Father-Wounds Shape Motherhood & How God Heals Them*

MAD AT DADDY Workbook: *Companion Workbook for Healing Father-Wounds*

PRAYERS FOR HEALING FATHER WOUNDS that affect Motherhood: *Prayer Manual*

Man Safari, *The*

Marriage Ed. Rules of Engagement & Marriage

Made Perfect in Love

Money Hunters: Beware of Those

Money on the Altar https://a.co/d/4EqJ2Nr

Mulberry Tree https://a.co/d/9nR9rRb

Motherboard (The) - *Soul Prosperity Series*

Name Your Seed

Occupy: *Until I Return*

One Defining Day: A Day When Dreams Come True

Plantation Souls

Players Gonna Play

Power Money: Nine Times the Tithe
https://a.co/d/gRt41gy

The Power of Wealth *(forthcoming)*

Powers Above

Repent of Visiting Evil Altars
https://a.co/d/3n3Zjwx

The Robe, *Part 1, The Lessons of Joseph*

The Robe, *The Lessons of Joseph* Part II,

Seasons of Grief

Seasons of Rest (forthcoming)

Seasons of Siege: GOD IS COMING

Seasons of Waiting

Seasons of War

Second Marriage, Third--, *Any Marriage*
https://a.co/d/6m6GN4N

Sift You Like Wheat

Six Men Short: What Has Happened to all the Men?

Soul Tie Series: 3 book series: *The Soul Tie Book,*
The Soul Tie Workbook, The Soul Tie Prayer Manual

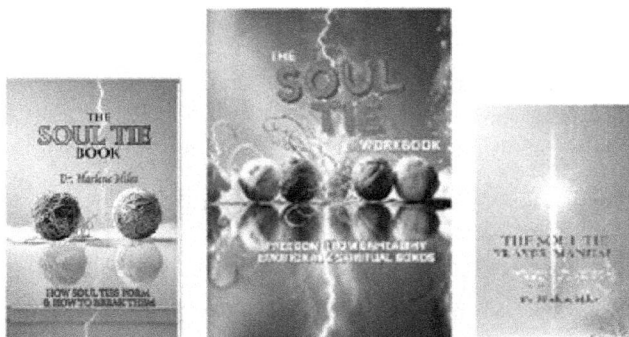

Soul Prosperity, Soul Prosperity Series Book 3
https://a.co/d/5p8YvCN

Souls Captivity, Soul Prosperity Series Book 2

The Spirit of Poverty

StarStruck

SUNBLOCK

The Swallowers: *Thieves of Darkness,* Bk 3

Take It Back

This Is NOT That: How to Keep Demons from Coming at You

Time Is of the Essence

Too Many Wives: *Why You Have Lady Problems*

Tormenting Spirits https://a.co/d/dAogEJf

Toxic Souls

Triangular Power *(series)*

- Powers Above
- SUNBLOCK
- Do Not Swear by the Moon
- STARSTRUCK

TRIBE: *What Covenants Govern You...?*

Uncontested Doom

Unguarded Hours, *The*

Unseen Life, *The* https://a.co/d/0drZ5Ll

Upgrade: How to Get Out of Survival Mode
Toxic Souls (Book 2 of series), Legacy (Book 3 of series),

The Wasters: *Thieves of Darkness,* Bk 2
https://a.co/d/bUvI9Jo

What Have You to Declare? What Do You Have With You from Where You've Been?

When I Was A Child, *I Prayed As a Child*

When the Devourer is Rebuked

https://a.co/d/1HVv8oq

The Wilderness Romance *(series)* This series is about conducting a Godly relationship and marriage with someone who is a Wilderness person. It is about how to recognize it and navigate through it. These books are about how not to get caught up in such.

- *The Social Wilderness*

- *The Sexual Wilderness*
- *The Spiritual Wilderness*

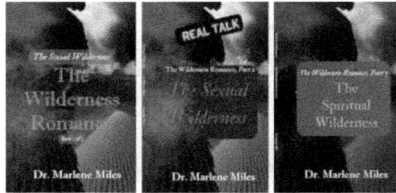

Other Series

The Fold (a series on Godly finances)
https://a.co/d/4hz3unj

Soul Prosperity Series https://a.co/d/bz2M42q

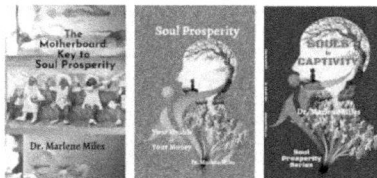

Spirit Spouse books

https://a.co/d/9VehDSo

https://a.co/d/97sKOwm

Thieves of Darkness series

Triangular Powers https://a.co/d/aUCjAWC

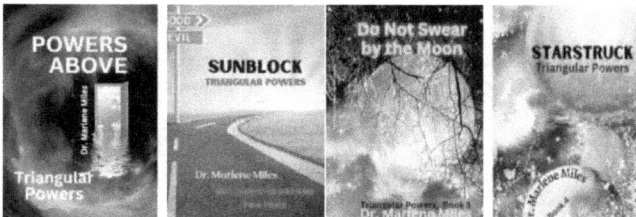

Upgrade (series) *How to Get Out of Survival Mode*
https://a.co/d/aTERhXO

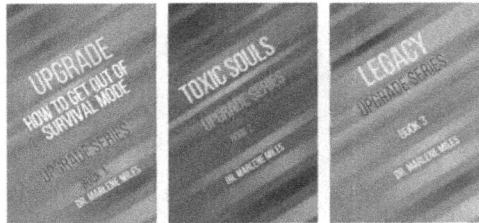

WE GET ALONG, RIGHT? *Compatibility Reality for Couples*

Companion Workbook: **WE GET ALONG, RIGHT?** *The Workbook for Couples Who Think They Do*

www.ingramcontent.com/pod-product-compliance
Lightning Source LLC
LaVergne TN
LVHW052028080426
835513LV00018B/2224